Cooking Light.

FISH & SHELLFISH
COOKBOOK

Cooking Light.

FISH & SHELLFISH
COOKBOOK

COMPILED AND EDITED BY
SUSAN M. MCINTOSH, M.S., R.D.

OXMOOR
HOUSE

ISBN: 0-8487-2725-X
Printed in the United States of America
First Printing 2002

Previously published as *Low-Fat Ways to Cook Fish & Shellfish*
  © 1997 by Oxmoor House, Inc.

Editor-in-Chief: Nancy Fitzpatrick Wyatt
Editorial Director, Special Interest Publications: Ann H. Harvey
Senior Foods Editor: Katherine M. Eakin
Senior Editor, Editorial Services: Olivia Kindig Wells
Art Director: James Boone

COOKING LIGHT® FISH & SHELLFISH COOKBOOK

Menu and Recipe Consultant: Susan McEwen McIntosh, M.S., R.D.
Assistant Editor: Kelly Hooper Troiano
Associate Foods Editor: Anne Chappell Cain, M.S., M.P.H., R.D.
Copy Editor: Shari K. Wimberly
Editorial Assistant: Kaye Howard Smith
Indexer: Mary Ann Laurens
Associate Art Director: Cynthia R. Cooper
Designer: Carol Damsky
Senior Photographer: Jim Bathie
Photographers: Howard L. Puckett, Ralph Anderson
Senior Photo Stylist: Kay E. Clarke
Photo Stylists: Cindy Manning Barr, Virginia R. Cravens
Production and Distribution Director: Phillip Lee
Associate Production Manager: Vanessa Cobbs Richardson

Cover: *Shrimp and Mussels Medley (recipe on page 104)*
Frontispiece: *Hickory-Grilled Amberjack with Grilled Salsa (recipe on page 108)*

To order additional publications, call 1-800-633-4910.

For more books to enrich your life, visit
oxmoorhouse.com

CONTENTS

FISH & SHELLFISH FACTS

*W*hen it comes to preparing quick, great-tasting entrées that are low in fat and calories, fish and shellfish are hard to beat. But if the thought of preparing orange roughy, salmon, or clams intimidates you, read on. You'll find all the information you need—from selection to storage to basic "how-to's."

Loaded with protein, vitamins, and minerals, yet low in fat, fish and shellfish are among the healthiest entrée choices around. Even the moderate amounts of fat found in some fish provide omega-3 fatty acids, the polyunsaturated fat that may help reduce the risk of heart disease.

In the next few pages, you will learn how to select, store, and prepare high-quality fish and shellfish. On page 9, you'll see how to tackle a lobster, and on page 10 you'll find a listing of appropriate seafood substitutions.

FISH

As you probably know already, it is imperative to start your food preparation with the freshest fish available in your locale.

• **Selection.** Purchase fresh fish from a reputable store that has a quick turnover and that regularly replenishes its stock. One of the best ways to judge freshness is by smell. Fish should have a mild smell, not an offensive, fishy odor.

Look for eyes that are clear, bright, and full or almost bulging. As a fish loses its freshness, the eyes become cloudy, pink, and sunken in appearance.

Check for firmness. The flesh should spring back when pressed lightly; if an indentation remains, do not buy the fish. Whole fresh fish should have shiny skin with firmly attached scales. The gills should be bright pinkish-red and not slimy.

Select fish steaks and fillets that are moist and freshly cut. Avoid pieces that are yellow or brown around the edges.

Commercially frozen fish has been flash-frozen to capture color, moisture, and flavor. It is an excellent choice for consumers if properly thawed.

Be sure frozen fish is wrapped in moisture- and vapor-resistant packaging and is solidly frozen with no discoloration or freezer burn. There should be little or no air within the wrapping. Ice crystals may indicate that the fish has been thawed and re-frozen, which can ruin it.

• **Market forms.** You can purchase fish in a variety of forms:

A *whole or round fish* is exactly as it comes from the water. It may need to be scaled, and it will need to be eviscerated, or gutted, before cooking.

A whole fish that has been eviscerated and scaled is referred to as a *drawn fish*.

A drawn fish with the head, fins, and sometimes the tail removed is referred to as *dressed*. Smaller fish that have been dressed are called *pan-dressed*.

The boneless sides of a fish that have been cut lengthwise away from the backbone are *fillets*.

Filleting a fish

Cross-sectional slices cut from large, dressed fish are called *steaks*. The slices usually measure ¾ to 1 inch thick and include the backbone and ribs.

Slicing a fish into steaks

• **Storage.** Cook fresh fish on the day of purchase for the best taste. But fish may be stored in the coldest part of the refrigerator for up to two days. Be sure to wrap it tightly in heavy-duty plastic wrap or freezer paper before storing. A damp cloth placed over the fish, inside the wrapping, will prevent the fish from drying out.

Freeze fresh fish within two days of purchase, and store it in the freezer for up to three months.

Return commercially frozen fish to the freezer as soon as possible after purchase.

Thaw frozen fish in the refrigerator, if possible. If you're in a hurry, place the frozen fish in a plastic bag under cold running water until thawed. Do not thaw frozen fish at room temperature. Drain and blot thawed fish with paper towels before cooking.

Do not thaw frozen breaded fish products before cooking; prepare these products according to the package directions. Cooked fish can be stored in the refrigerator for two days.

• **Preparation.** Dry heat methods (broiling, grilling, and sautéing) are considered better for cooking fish that are higher in fat, while leaner fish remain more moist when cooked by moist heat methods (microwaving, oven-frying, poaching, and steaming). If you do cook lean fish by a dry heat method, you will want to baste frequently. (Refer to the chart on page 10 to determine the fat content of various types of fish).

Avoid overcooking fish and cooking at too high a temperature. Both cause the fish to be tough and dry. Check the fish occasionally for doneness while cooking. To test for doneness, pierce the thickest part of the fish with a fork, and twist the fork; most fish will flake easily when done. It will also lose its transparency and become opaque.

The Safety Question

Eating raw seafood, especially oysters, may be risky to your health. Raw oysters may contain a bacterium that can cause serious illness in people with certain medical conditions. Cooking the oysters kills the bacterium.

Another concern is that some fish absorb and store mercury and other contaminants from the water in which they live. Cooking does not destroy these contaminants. You should not be concerned about most fish, but it's recommended that you limit your consumption of swordfish, shark, and other large predatory fish to about one serving a week.

Call the Food and Drug Administration's Seafood Hotline at 800-332-4010 for 24-hour recorded information if you have questions about seafood safety.

SHELLFISH

Freshness is as important with shellfish as it is with fish. Once removed from the water, shellfish begin to deteriorate quickly.

• **Selection.** Many types of shellfish are kept alive in water tanks or on beds of ice until purchased; some are also available fresh-cooked, frozen, or frozen-cooked.

The keys to perfect shellfish are to buy it fresh, keep it cold, and use it quickly.

You can purchase oysters, mussels, and hard-shelled clams live in the shell. The shells should be tightly closed and unbroken. If a shell is open and doesn't close when you touch it, the shellfish is dead and should be discarded. Shells that are heavy or broken may be filled with sand.

An exception is the soft-shelled clam, which doesn't close completely when fresh because of a protruding long, rubbery neck. If you touch the neck, it should move; if it does not, you should discard the clam. The most common soft-shell clam is the steamer clam on the East Coast and the razor clam on the West Coast.

Oysters and clams are also available shucked and fresh or shucked and canned. If they are fresh, shucked, and in their liquor, don't discard the liquor; it contains a lot of flavor that you can add to the recipe. Keep in mind that the liquor should be more clear than milky.

Large sea scallops are the more common type of scallop. Bay scallops, which have a sweeter, more delicate flavor, are smaller and usually more tender.

When substituting sea scallops for bay scallops, cut them into quarters or in thin slices.

Scallops are usually shucked immediately after harvest. They should have little liquor around them and should have a slightly sweet odor. Rinse shucked scallops well before cooking, as sand accumulates in the crevices.

Purchase whole lobsters and crabs alive and keep them alive until you are ready to cook them. Look for lobsters that are moving and that curl their tails when lifted from the water. Live crabs should also move energetically when purchased. Fresh cooked crabmeat should have little smell and should be used within two days of purchase.

Fresh raw shrimp vary in color from greenish-gray to pink, indicating the type of water the shrimp came from, not their quality. All shrimp will turn pale pink during cooking. The flesh should feel firm and slippery, and fresh shrimp should have a mild, sweet smell. An odor of ammonia indicates that the shrimp are old.

• **Storage.** Store live clams, mussels, and oysters in their shells in the coldest part of the refrigerator for up to two days for the freshest taste. Place them in a large container, and cover with a damp cloth. Do not store them in an airtight container because they will suffocate. If any shells open during storage, tap them and discard any that don't close quickly.

Store shucked clams, mussels, oysters, and scallops covered in their own juices in the refrigerator for up to two days. You can also freeze them for up to three months. But make sure that they are covered in their juices to prevent freezer burn; you may need to add extra water.

Crabs and lobsters are best when cooked on the day of purchase. To store until cooking time, place the crabs or lobsters in a pan or bowl, cover with a damp towel, and place in the coldest part of the refrigerator. Once you cook the shellfish, use its meat within a day or two, or wrap it tightly and freeze for up to three months.

Rinse fresh raw shrimp under cold running water, and drain well. Store in a tightly covered container in the refrigerator for two to three days. Store cooked shrimp in the refrigerator for up to two days. You can freeze fresh shrimp for up to five months.

Seafood has a limited storage life in home freezers. Be sure to label and date any seafood that you freeze.

SHELLFISH: STEP-BY-STEP PREPARATION

OYSTERS

 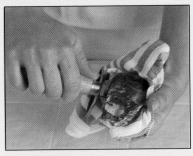 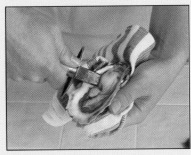

1. Grip oyster with hinge away from you and flatter shell on top. Insert oyster knife into hinge, and twist to pry open shell.

2. Slide knife along inside of the flatter shell to cut the muscle. Discard top shell.

3. To shuck oyster, run the tip of the knife around the bottom shell to loosen oyster. Discard any broken shell pieces.

LOBSTER

 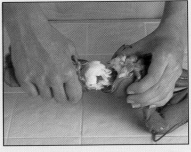 

1. Grasp a live lobster behind the head with your hand or long tongs, and plunge it into boiling water. Return to a boil; cover, reduce heat, and simmer 10 minutes.

2. The cooked lobster will be red. Drain; let cool. Hold by ends so the underside faces up. Bend until tail separates from body.

3. Cut the flippers from the tail; push with your thumb where they were attached. Gently pull the meat out of the other end. Cut off and discard the intestinal vein.

SHRIMP

 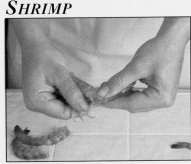 

4. Gently remove pincer on claw. Use a lobster cracker or mallet to crack the shell of claws. Pull apart to remove meat. Use a fork or skewer to remove any other meat.

1. Pinch heads from shrimp, if still attached. Grasp tail in one hand and legs in the other. Pull off legs and back shell.

2. Make a slit along back of the shrimp with a sharp paring knife; remove the intestinal vein. Remove tail, if desired.

SEAFOOD SUBSTITUTIONS

What if your fish market has a sale on grouper but the recipe you've selected calls for halibut? Or perhaps your recipe calls for flounder, but flounder is not readily available in your part of the country. Go ahead and make a substitution.

Knowing what alternatives are workable allows you to purchase seafood in season, at lower prices and peak quality. The following seafood are grouped according to similar flavor and texture. Fish and shellfish in each category taste somewhat alike and can often be prepared the same way. (Substitute fish for fish, shellfish for shellfish.) Finfish are listed first within each category, followed by shellfish, when appropriate.

It is usually best to use the same market form when making substitutions. For example, if the recipe calls for flounder fillets, you might use sole fillets but not a whole fish.

Delicate texture
- Mild flavor: cod, flounder, haddock, pollock, sole, crab, scallops
- Moderate flavor: lake perch, whitefish, whiting
- Full flavor: mussels, oysters

Moderate texture
- Mild flavor: orange roughy, pike, tilapia, crawfish, lobster, shrimp
- Moderate flavor: mullet, ocean perch, trout, sea trout
- Full flavor: bluefish, mackerel

Firm texture
- Mild flavor: grouper, halibut, monkfish, sea bass, snapper, tilefish
- Moderate flavor: amberjack, catfish, mahimahi, pompano, shark
- Full flavor: marlin, salmon, swordfish, tuna, clams

FISH AND SHELLFISH NUTRIENTS

Fish or Shellfish (3 ounces cooked)	Calories	Fat (grams)	Cholesterol (milligrams)
Fish			
Bass, striped	105	2.5	88
Catfish, freshwater	132	4.8	66
Cod	89	0.7	47
Flounder	100	1.3	58
Grouper	100	1.1	40
Haddock	95	0.8	63
Halibut	119	2.5	35
Mackerel, Spanish	134	5.4	62
Mahimahi	93	0.8	80
Monkfish	82	1.7	27
Orange roughy	76	0.8	22
Perch	100	1.0	98
Pollock	100	1.1	77
Pompano	179	10.3	54
Red snapper	109	1.5	40
Salmon			
Caho	157	6.4	42
Sockeye	184	9.3	74
Scamp	100	1.1	40
Sole	100	1.3	58
Swordfish	132	4.4	43
Trout, rainbow	128	3.7	62
Tuna			
White, canned in water, drained	116	2.1	36
Yellowfin	118	1.0	49
Whitefish	146	6.4	65
Shellfish			
Clams	126	1.7	57
Crab			
Alaskan king	82	1.3	45
Blue	87	1.5	85
Dungeness	94	1.1	65
Crawfish	97	1.1	151
Lobster	83	0.5	61
Mussels	146	3.8	48
Oysters	117	4.2	93
Scallops	100	0.9	37
Shrimp	84	0.9	166

LOW-FAT BASICS

*W*hether you are trying to lose or maintain weight, low-fat eating makes good sense. Research studies show that decreasing your fat intake reduces risks of heart disease, diabetes, and some types of cancer. The goal recommended by major health groups is an intake of 30 percent or less of total daily calories.

The *Cooking Light Fish and Shellfish Cookbook* helps you meet that goal. It gives you practical, delicious recipes with realistic advice about low-fat cooking and eating. The recipes are lower in total fat than traditional recipes, and most provide less than 30 percent of calories from fat and less than 10 percent from saturated fat.

Some types of fish and shellfish, however, naturally derive more than 30 percent of calories from fat, even though the fish or shellfish is considered lean. With such fish we have added little, if any, fat in order to keep the percentage of calories from fat as low as possible. For example, in the Fourth of July Cookout on page 17 the swordfish scales in at 37 percent fat, but when combined with the rest of the menu, the meal provides only 27 percent fat.

The goal of fat reduction is not to eliminate fat entirely. In fact, some fat is needed to transport fat-soluble vitamins and maintain other body functions.

FIGURING THE FAT

The easiest way to achieve a diet with 30 percent or fewer of total calories from fat is to establish a daily "fat budget" based on the total number of calories you need each day. To estimate your daily calorie requirements, multiply your current weight by 15. Remember that this is only a rough guide because calorie requirements vary according to age, body size, and level of activity. To gain or lose 1 pound a week, add or subtract 500 calories a day. (A diet of fewer than 1,200 calories a day is not recommended unless medically supervised.)

Once you determine your calorie requirement, it's easy to figure the number of fat grams you should consume each day. These should equal or be lower than the number of fat grams indicated on the Daily Fat Limits chart.

DAILY FAT LIMITS		
Calories Per Day	30 Percent of Calories	Grams of Fat
1,200	360	40
1,500	450	50
1,800	540	60
2,000	600	67
2,200	660	73
2,500	750	83
2,800	840	93

NUTRITIONAL ANALYSIS

Each recipe in *Cooking Light Fish and Shellfish Cookbook* has been kitchen-tested by a staff of qualified home economists. In addition, registered dietitians have determined the nutrient information, using a computer system to analyze every ingredient. These efforts ensure the success of each recipe and will help you fit these recipes into your own meal planning.

The nutrient grid that follows each recipe provides calories per serving and the percentage of calories from fat. Also, the grid lists the grams of total fat, saturated fat, protein, and carbohydrate, and the milligrams of cholesterol and sodium per serving. The nutrient values are as accurate as possible and are based on these assumptions.

• When the recipe calls for cooked pasta, rice, or noodles, we base the analysis on cooking without additional salt or fat.

• Only the amount of marinade absorbed by the food is calculated.

• Garnishes and other optional ingredients are not calculated.

• Some of the alcohol calories evaporate during heating, and only those remaining are calculated.

• When a range is given for an ingredient (3 to 3½ cups, for instance), we calculate the lesser amount.

• Fruits and vegetables listed in the ingredients are not peeled unless specified.

Baked Halibut Provençal, Green Beans with Basil, and Oven-Roasted Potato Slices (menu on page 20)

SENSIBLE DINNERS

*T*he word is out—most fish and shellfish are low in fat and high in nutritional value. What's more, you can cook fish and shellfish quickly, enabling you to get in and out of the kitchen in a hurry. So don't hesitate to include these delicacies in your menu plans.

If you want suggestions for what to serve with your main course, just flip through the following pages to find ideas for a casual seafood supper (page 14), a festive Fourth of July Cookout (page 17), or an elegant fish dinner for two (page 20). Try the side dishes and desserts featured in the menus with many other fish and shellfish recipes in this book.

SEAFOOD SUPPER IN A SNAP

Dinner at the snap of a finger? Not quite, but there's no doubt that this menu is easy to prepare. The key is timing.

Make the dessert the day before, and chill until ready to serve after the dinner. Slice the plum tomatoes to accompany the amberjack fillets; then prepare the rice. As the rice cooks, finish preparing and baking the fish. Spend the last few minutes steaming the broccoli and warming the dinner rolls (one per person).

Seasoned Fish and Tomatoes

Spicy Yellow Rice

Broccoli Vinaigrette

Commercial whole wheat dinner rolls

Raspberry Cream Pie

Serves 6
TOTAL CALORIES PER SERVING: 509
(CALORIES FROM FAT: 23%)

SEASONED FISH AND TOMATOES

6 (4-ounce) amberjack fillets
1 teaspoon dried oregano
½ teaspoon cracked pepper
6 plum tomatoes, cut into ¼-inch-thick slices
Vegetable cooking spray
¾ cup dry white wine
2 tablespoons sliced ripe olives
Fresh oregano sprigs (optional)
Whole peppercorns (optional)

Sprinkle fillets with oregano and cracked pepper. Place fillets and tomato in a 13- x 9- x 2-inch baking dish coated with cooking spray. Add wine.

Bake, uncovered, at 350° for 15 minutes or until fish flakes easily when tested with a fork.

To serve, place tomato slices evenly on individual serving plates, using a slotted spoon. Top each serving with a fillet and 1 teaspoon olives. If desired, garnish each serving with a fresh oregano sprig and whole peppercorns. Yield: 6 servings.

PER SERVING: 142 CALORIES (20% FROM FAT)
FAT 3.2G (SATURATED FAT 0.8G)
PROTEIN 24.6G   CARBOHYDRATE 3.4G
CHOLESTEROL 49MG   SODIUM 95MG

Seasoned Fish and Tomatoes, Spicy Yellow Rice, and Broccoli Vinaigrette

SPICY YELLOW RICE

Vegetable cooking spray
1¼ cups chopped onion
¾ cup uncooked long-grain rice
1¾ cups plus 2 tablespoons water
¾ teaspoon ground turmeric
½ teaspoon hot sauce
¼ teaspoon salt
¼ teaspoon garlic powder
¼ teaspoon pepper
1 bay leaf

Coat a large nonstick skillet with cooking spray; place over medium-high heat until hot. Add onion, and sauté until tender. Add rice, stirring gently. Add water and remaining ingredients; bring to a boil. Cover, reduce heat, and simmer 22 minutes or until rice is tender and liquid is absorbed. Remove and discard bay leaf. Yield: 6 (½-cup) servings.

PER SERVING: 104 CALORIES (3% FROM FAT)
FAT 0.4G (SATURATED FAT 0.1G)
PROTEIN 2.2G CARBOHYDRATE 22.6G
CHOLESTEROL 0MG SODIUM 103MG

BROCCOLI VINAIGRETTE

1½ pounds fresh broccoli
2 tablespoons balsamic vinegar
1 teaspoon Dijon mustard
½ teaspoon olive oil
¼ teaspoon pepper
⅛ teaspoon salt

Trim off large leaves of broccoli, and remove tough ends of lower stalks. Wash broccoli; cut into spears. Arrange in a steamer basket over boiling water. Cover; steam 5 minutes or until crisp-tender. Drain; transfer to a serving platter, and keep warm.

Combine vinegar and remaining 4 ingredients, stirring well with a wire whisk. Drizzle vinegar mixture over broccoli. Yield: 6 servings.

PER SERVING: 22 CALORIES (29% FROM FAT)
FAT 0.7G (SATURATED FAT 0.1G)
PROTEIN 1.9G CARBOHYDRATE 3.5G
CHOLESTEROL 0MG SODIUM 91MG

RASPBERRY CREAM PIE

½ cup graham cracker crumbs
¼ cup finely chopped pecans
3 tablespoons reduced-calorie margarine, melted
1 tablespoon sugar
1 (12-ounce) package frozen raspberries in light syrup, thawed
1 envelope unflavored gelatin
¼ cup cold water
¼ teaspoon grated lime rind
1 tablespoon fresh lime juice
1 (8-ounce) carton raspberry low-fat yogurt
1 cup frozen reduced-calorie whipped topping, thawed
Lime slices (optional)

Combine first 4 ingredients in a small bowl, stirring well. Press mixture into bottom and halfway up sides of a 9-inch pieplate. Bake at 350° for 8 to 10 minutes or until golden. Remove from oven, and let cool on a wire rack.

Place raspberries in container of an electric blender; cover and process until smooth. Pour raspberry puree through a wire-mesh strainer; press with back of spoon against the sides of the strainer to squeeze out juice. Discard remaining pulp and seeds in strainer.

Sprinkle gelatin over cold water in a small non-aluminum saucepan; let stand 1 minute. Cook over low heat, stirring constantly, until gelatin dissolves. Remove from heat, and stir in reserved raspberry puree, lime rind, and lime juice. Chill until the consistency of unbeaten egg white.

Add yogurt, and stir well. Gently fold in whipped topping. Spoon mixture into prepared pie crust. Cover and chill at least 2 hours. Garnish with lime slices, if desired. Yield: 8 servings.

PER SERVING: 169 CALORIES (38% FROM FAT)
FAT 7.1G (SATURATED FAT 1.5G)
PROTEIN 3.0G CARBOHYDRATE 24.8G
CHOLESTEROL 1MG SODIUM 98MG

Herb-Grilled Swordfish, Zesty Corn Salad, and Tangy Marinated Tomatoes

FOURTH OF JULY COOKOUT

You won't miss the fireworks fun with this menu because you can do most of the work ahead. On the morning of the party, prepare the corn, tomatoes, and sorbet. Once the guests arrive, grill the swordfish, heat the bread, and enjoy a delicious spread.

Herb-Grilled Swordfish

Zesty Corn Salad

Tangy Marinated Tomatoes

Seasoned Italian Bread

Watermelon Sorbet

Serves 6
TOTAL CALORIES PER SERVING: 582
(CALORIES FROM FAT: 27%)

HERB-GRILLED SWORDFISH

¼ cup unsweetened orange juice
3 tablespoons minced onion
1 tablespoon chopped fresh thyme
1 tablespoon chopped fresh basil
2 tablespoons low-sodium soy sauce
1½ tablespoons fresh lemon juice
1 tablespoon olive oil
½ teaspoon sugar
⅛ teaspoon salt
⅛ teaspoon pepper
1 clove garlic, minced
6 (4-ounce) swordfish steaks (½ inch thick)
Vegetable cooking spray
Fresh basil sprigs (optional)

Combine first 11 ingredients in a large heavy-duty, zip-top plastic bag. Add swordfish steaks; seal bag, and shake until steaks are well coated. Marinate in refrigerator 2 hours, turning bag occasionally.

Remove steaks from marinade, reserving marinade. Place marinade in a small saucepan. Bring to a boil; boil 1 minute.

Coat grill rack with cooking spray. Place on grill over medium-hot coals (350° to 400°). Place swordfish steaks on rack; grill, covered, 3 to 4 minutes on each side or until fish flakes easily when tested with a fork, basting occasionally with marinade. Garnish swordfish steaks with fresh basil sprigs, if desired. Yield: 6 servings.

PER SERVING: 165 CALORIES (37% FROM FAT)
FAT 6.8G (SATURATED FAT 1.5G)
PROTEIN 21.8G   CARBOHYDRATE 2.5G
CHOLESTEROL 43MG   SODIUM 277MG

ZESTY CORN SALAD

4 cups fresh corn cut from cob (about 8 ears)
1 cup water
1⅓ cups chopped sweet red pepper
1 cup sliced celery
½ cup sliced green onions
½ cup chopped fresh parsley
½ cup chopped fresh basil
½ cup raspberry wine vinegar
¼ cup sugar
1 tablespoon vegetable oil
½ teaspoon salt
¼ teaspoon pepper

Combine corn kernels and water in a medium saucepan, and bring to a boil. Reduce heat, and simmer, uncovered, 15 minutes or until corn is tender. Drain well.

Combine cooked corn, sweet red pepper, celery, green onions, parsley, and basil in a medium bowl.

Combine vinegar, sugar, oil, salt, and pepper in a small bowl, stirring well. Pour vinegar mixture over corn mixture, and toss well. Cover and chill at least 8 hours, stirring occasionally. Toss gently before serving. Yield: 6 (1-cup) servings.

PER SERVING: 165 CALORIES (26% FROM FAT)
FAT 4.8G (SATURATED FAT 0.8G)
PROTEIN 3.8G   CARBOHYDRATE 31.4G
CHOLESTEROL 0MG   SODIUM 230MG

Tips on Herbs

If you don't have the fresh herb called for in a recipe, don't despair—you can usually substitute the dried form. Use about one-third as much of the dried herb as recommended for fresh.

And don't throw out a single leaf of any leftover fresh herbs. After you rinse the leaves with water, pat them dry and place them on a baking sheet to freeze. Once the leaves are frozen, store them in freezer bags to use in cooking.

TANGY MARINATED TOMATOES

3 large tomatoes, cut into ¼-inch-thick slices
2 tablespoons sliced green onions
1 tablespoon chopped fresh parsley
1 tablespoon chopped fresh basil
¼ cup plus 2 tablespoons red wine vinegar
1 tablespoon olive oil
½ teaspoon salt
¼ teaspoon sugar
¼ teaspoon pepper
1 clove garlic, minced
Lettuce leaves (optional)

Place tomato slices in a large shallow dish.
Combine green onions and next 8 ingredients in a small jar; cover tightly, and shake vigorously. Pour over tomato slices. Cover and marinate in refrigerator at least 2 hours. Transfer tomatoes to a lettuce-lined serving platter, if desired. Yield: 6 servings.

PER SERVING: 55 CALORIES (46% FROM FAT)
FAT 2.8G (SATURATED FAT 0.4G)
PROTEIN 1.3G CARBOHYDRATE 7.8G
CHOLESTEROL 0MG SODIUM 209MG

SEASONED ITALIAN BREAD

You may heat this bread, wrapped in foil, on the grill rack while the fish cooks.

½ (16-ounce) loaf unsliced Italian bread
1 tablespoon grated Parmesan cheese
1 tablespoon reduced-calorie margarine, melted
1½ teaspoons olive oil
½ teaspoon dried Italian seasoning
⅛ teaspoon onion powder
⅛ teaspoon garlic powder

Slice bread crosswise into 6 slices, cutting to, but not through, bottom of loaf; set aside.
Combine cheese and remaining 5 ingredients; spread over cut sides of bread, and wrap in aluminum foil.
Bake at 400° for 15 minutes or until thoroughly heated. Yield: 6 servings.

PER SERVING: 129 CALORIES (20% FROM FAT)
FAT 2.9G (SATURATED FAT 0.5G)
PROTEIN 3.8G CARBOHYDRATE 21.6G
CHOLESTEROL 1MG SODIUM 255MG

WATERMELON SORBET

10 cups seeded, cubed watermelon
⅔ cup sugar
1½ cups unsweetened apple juice
½ cup lemon juice
Fresh mint sprigs (optional)

Position knife blade in food processor bowl; add watermelon. Process until smooth. Transfer to a large bowl; add sugar, apple juice, and lemon juice, stirring well.
Pour watermelon mixture into freezer can of a 1-gallon hand-turned or electric freezer. Freeze according to manufacturer's instructions. Pack freezer with additional ice and rock salt, and let stand 1 hour before serving.
Scoop sorbet into individual dessert bowls. Garnish with fresh mint sprigs, if desired. Serve immediately. Yield: 20 (½-cup) servings.

PER SERVING: 68 CALORIES (5% FROM FAT)
FAT 0.4G (SATURATED FAT 0.2G)
PROTEIN 0.6G CARBOHYDRATE 16.4G
CHOLESTEROL 0MG SODIUM 3MG

A TASTE OF PROVENCE
(pictured on page 12)

Travel to sun-drenched Provence without leaving your kitchen. This menu highlights some of the French region's foods such as seafood, tomatoes, and oranges.

Make the orange dessert ahead to allow it time to chill. Cook the green beans while the fish and potatoes roast in the oven. Because this meal can be prepared with little effort, you'll have more time to visit with your special guest.

Baked Halibut Provençal

Oven-Roasted Potato Slices

Green Beans with Basil

Orange Slices with Grand Marnier

Serves 2
TOTAL CALORIES PER SERVING: 591
(CALORIES FROM FAT: 16%)

BAKED HALIBUT PROVENÇAL

1 small onion, thinly sliced
1 teaspoon olive oil
½ teaspoon dried rosemary, divided
1 small clove garlic, thinly sliced
1 (1½-inch) piece orange peel
¾ cup canned no-salt-added whole tomatoes, undrained and chopped
1 teaspoon capers
2 teaspoons unsweetened orange juice
⅛ teaspoon freshly ground pepper
2 (4-ounce) halibut fillets
2 teaspoons chopped kalamata olives
Fresh basil sprigs (optional)
Fresh rosemary sprigs (optional)

Combine onion, olive oil, ¼ teaspoon rosemary, garlic, and orange peel in a 13- x 9- x 2-inch baking dish. Bake, uncovered, at 400° for 10 minutes or until onion begins to brown, stirring once. Stir in tomatoes and capers; bake 5 additional minutes or until mixture thickens. Stir in orange juice and pepper.

Add halibut to tomato mixture; sprinkle with remaining ¼ teaspoon rosemary. Spoon tomato mixture over halibut; bake, uncovered, 10 minutes or until fish flakes easily when tested with a fork. Remove and discard orange peel. Sprinkle with olives. If desired, garnish with basil and rosemary sprigs. Yield: 2 servings.

PER SERVING: 194 CALORIES (25% FROM FAT)
FAT 5.4G (SATURATED FAT 0.8G)
PROTEIN 32.4G   CARBOHYDRATE 10.6G
CHOLESTEROL 53MG   SODIUM 216MG

OVEN-ROASTED POTATO SLICES

¾ pound baking potatoes, cut into ¼-inch-
　　thick slices
1 tablespoon balsamic vinegar
1 teaspoon olive oil
Olive oil-flavored vegetable cooking spray
⅛ teaspoon salt
⅛ teaspoon freshly ground pepper

Combine potato, vinegar, and oil in a medium bowl, tossing well.

Arrange potato in a single layer on a baking sheet coated with cooking spray. Bake at 400° for 30 minutes or until tender, turning once. Sprinkle with salt and pepper. Yield: 2 servings.

PER SERVING: 209 CALORIES (12% FROM FAT)
FAT 2.8G (SATURATED FAT 0.4G)
PROTEIN 3.8G   CARBOHYDRATE 43.1G
CHOLESTEROL 0MG   SODIUM 160MG

GREEN BEANS WITH BASIL

½ pound fresh green beans, trimmed
1 clove garlic, halved
¼ cup chopped fresh basil
1 teaspoon olive oil
⅛ teaspoon salt
⅛ teaspoon freshly ground pepper

Cook beans in boiling water to cover 8 minutes or until crisp-tender; drain well.

Rub the surface of a large bowl with cut sides of garlic. Leave garlic in bowl. Add basil and olive oil to bowl. Add beans, and toss well. Sprinkle with salt and pepper; toss. Remove and discard garlic halves. Yield: 2 servings.

PER SERVING: 54 CALORIES (40% FROM FAT)
FAT 2.4G (SATURATED FAT 0.3G)
PROTEIN 2.1G   CARBOHYDRATE 7.8G
CHOLESTEROL 0MG   SODIUM 153MG

ORANGE SLICES WITH GRAND MARNIER

2 large seedless oranges, peeled
2 teaspoons sugar
2 tablespoons Grand Marnier or other orange-
　　flavored liqueur
⅛ teaspoon ground cinnamon
Orange zest (optional)

Cut oranges into ¼-inch-thick slices. Place orange slices in individual bowls; sprinkle with sugar. Drizzle with Grand Marnier, and sprinkle with cinnamon. Cover and chill thoroughly. Garnish with orange zest, if desired. Yield: 2 servings.

PER SERVING: 134 CALORIES (1% FROM FAT)
FAT 0.2G (SATURATED FAT 0.1G)
PROTEIN 1.4G   CARBOHYDRATE 26.0G
CHOLESTEROL 0MG   SODIUM 0MG

Orange Slices with Grand Marnier

BACKYARD BEACH PARTY

It's summertime! Bring the beach to your own back door with this great-tasting menu and a few simple props like beach balls, lounge chairs, and splashy beach music. Prepare most of the meal early in the day, grilling the kabobs after guests arrive. (Menu reflects 2 cups cubed melon and one slice of bread per person.)

Skewered Shrimp and Sausage

Spicy Slaw

Honeydew cubes

Commercial French bread

Caramel-Brownie Chunk Ice Cream

Orange-Lemon Tea

Serves 10
TOTAL CALORIES PER SERVING: 786
(CALORIES FROM FAT: 17%)

Skewered Shrimp and Sausage and Orange-Lemon Tea

SKEWERED SHRIMP AND SAUSAGE

2 pounds unpeeled large fresh shrimp
⅔ cup canned no-salt-added chicken broth, undiluted
½ cup lemon juice
2 tablespoons chopped fresh parsley
1½ tablespoons minced onion
1½ tablespoons white wine Worcestershire sauce
1 tablespoon olive oil
1½ teaspoons sugar
½ teaspoon hot sauce
5 small round red potatoes, each cut into 4 wedges
5 ears fresh corn, each cut into 4 pieces
1 pound smoked turkey sausage, cut into 1½-inch pieces
Vegetable cooking spray

Peel and devein shrimp, leaving tails intact. Set shrimp aside.

Combine chicken broth and next 7 ingredients in a small bowl, stirring well; set aside half of chicken broth mixture. Pour remaining half of chicken broth mixture into a large heavy-duty, zip-top plastic bag. Add shrimp and potato wedges; seal bag, and shake until shrimp and potato wedges are well coated. Marinate in refrigerator 2 to 3 hours, turning bag occasionally.

Remove shrimp and potato from marinade, discarding marinade. Thread shrimp on 4 (14-inch) skewers. Thread potato, corn, and sausage separately on 6 (14-inch) skewers.

Coat grill rack with cooking spray; place on grill over medium-hot coals (350° to 400°). Place potato kabobs on rack, and grill, covered, 10 minutes.

While potato kabobs continue to cook, add corn and sausage kabobs to rack; grill, covered, 10 minutes or until potato and corn are tender and sausage is thoroughly heated, turning and basting occasionally with reserved chicken broth mixture. Remove potato, corn, and sausage kabobs from grill.

Place shrimp on rack; grill 3 to 4 minutes on each side or until shrimp turn pink, basting frequently with reserved chicken broth mixture.

Remove corn, potatoes, sausage, and shrimp from skewers, and place each in individual groups on a large serving platter. Yield: 10 servings.

PER SERVING: 245 CALORIES (32% FROM FAT)
FAT 8.7G (SATURATED FAT 2.5G)
PROTEIN 20.8G   CARBOHYDRATE 22.1G
CHOLESTEROL 130MG   SODIUM 528MG

SPICY SLAW

To save time, chop the vegetables in the food processor or substitute preshredded coleslaw mix for the green and red cabbage.

4 cups shredded green cabbage
4 cups shredded red cabbage
1 cup chopped green pepper
1 cup shredded carrot
⅔ cup chopped onion
⅔ cup low-sodium light and tangy vegetable juice
¼ cup white vinegar
1 tablespoon sugar
1 tablespoon vegetable oil
1 teaspoon chili powder
½ teaspoon salt
2 jalapeño peppers, seeded and minced
5 medium-size ripe tomatoes, thinly sliced

Combine first 5 ingredients in a large bowl, and set aside.

Combine vegetable juice and next 6 ingredients in a small bowl, stirring well. Pour juice mixture over cabbage mixture, and toss well. Cover and marinate in refrigerator at least 2 hours, tossing occasionally.

To serve, line a large platter with tomato slices. Spoon cabbage mixture evenly over tomato slices, using a slotted spoon. Yield: 10 servings.

PER SERVING: 64 CALORIES (27% FROM FAT)
FAT 1.9G (SATURATED FAT 0.3G)
PROTEIN 1.9G   CARBOHYDRATE 11.7G
CHOLESTEROL 0MG   SODIUM 142MG

CARAMEL-BROWNIE CHUNK ICE CREAM

½ (20½-ounce) package light fudge brownie
    mix (about 2 cups)
¼ cup water
1 egg white, lightly beaten
Vegetable cooking spray
1 (14-ounce) can low-fat sweetened condensed
    milk
¼ cup sugar
¼ cup all-purpose flour
3 cups 1% low-fat milk
2 (12-ounce) cans evaporated skimmed milk
2 egg yolks, lightly beaten

Combine one-half package brownie mix, water, and egg white in a bowl, stirring well. Reserve remaining brownie mix for another use. Spread mixture into an 8-inch square pan coated with cooking spray. Bake at 350° for 20 to 22 minutes or just until done (do not overbake). Let cool on a wire rack.

Place sweetened condensed milk in a 9-inch pieplate. Cover pieplate with aluminum foil. Place pieplate in a larger shallow pan. Add hot water to pan to depth of ¼ inch. Bake at 425° for 1 hour and 20 minutes or until sweetened condensed milk is thick and caramel colored. (Add hot water to pan as needed.) Remove aluminum foil, and let caramelized milk cool.

Combine sugar and flour in a large saucepan, stirring well. Gradually add low-fat and evaporated milks, stirring until smooth. Cook over medium heat, stirring constantly, until thickened (about 15 minutes). Gradually stir one-fourth of hot mixture into beaten egg yolks; add to remaining hot mixture, stirring constantly. Cook over medium heat, stirring constantly, 1 minute. Remove from heat; stir in caramelized milk. Let cool. Chill thoroughly.

Pour caramelized milk mixture into freezer can of a 1-gallon hand-turned or electric freezer. Freeze according to manufacturer's instructions. Cut cooled brownie into ½-inch cubes. Stir brownie cubes into ice cream. Pack freezer with additional ice and rock salt; let stand 1 hour before serving. Yield: 18 (½-cup) servings.

Note: Store remaining brownie mix in a heavy-duty, zip-top plastic bag in refrigerator; reserved brownie mix can be used to repeat this procedure or to make a small pan of brownies.

PER SERVING: 203 CALORIES (14% FROM FAT)
FAT 3.2G (SATURATED FAT 1.3G)
PROTEIN 7.5G   CARBOHYDRATE 36.2G
CHOLESTEROL 30MG   SODIUM 145MG

ORANGE-LEMON TEA

6 regular-size tea bags
3 cups boiling water
½ cup sugar
1½ quarts cold water
1 (6-ounce) can frozen orange juice
    concentrate, thawed and undiluted
½ (6-ounce) can frozen lemonade concentrate,
    thawed and undiluted
Lemon slices (optional)
Orange slices (optional)

Combine tea bags and boiling water. Cover and let steep 5 minutes. Remove and discard tea bags.

Combine tea, sugar, cold water, orange juice concentrate, and lemonade concentrate, stirring well; cover and chill. Serve over ice. If desired, garnish with lemon and orange slices. Yield: 10 (1-cup) servings.

PER SERVING: 82 CALORIES (1% FROM FAT)
FAT 0.1G (SATURATED FAT 0.0G)
PROTEIN 0.4G   CARBOHYDRATE 20.7G
CHOLESTEROL 0MG   SODIUM 3MG

Quick Spritzers

For another refreshing beverage, combine equal parts of chilled unsweetened fruit juice (apple, orange, or white grape juice) and sparkling mineral water. Serve this easy spritzer with a slice of lemon or lime and a sprig of fresh mint.

ENGAGEMENT PARTY BUFFET

Celebrate the engagement of a loving couple with this easy, elegant buffet. It features a rich-tasting shrimp and crab lasagna and a unique green salad. For dessert, offer old-fashioned tea cakes with cappuccino. (Analysis includes one roll and one cookie per serving.)

Seafood Lasagna

Lemon Squash

Mixed Greens with Walnut Vinaigrette

Commercial French rolls

Orange Marmalade Tea Cakes

Mocha Cappuccino

Serves 8
TOTAL CALORIES PER SERVING: 717
(CALORIES FROM FAT: 26%)

Seafood Lasagna, Mixed Greens with Walnut Vinaigrette, and Lemon Squash

SEAFOOD LASAGNA

2 (10-ounce) packages frozen chopped
    spinach, thawed
6 cups water
1¼ pounds unpeeled small fresh shrimp
Vegetable cooking spray
½ cup chopped onion
½ cup chopped green pepper
2 cloves garlic, minced
1 (8-ounce) package Neufchâtel cheese
1 (16-ounce) container 1% low-fat cottage
    cheese
¾ cup (3 ounces) shredded reduced-fat Swiss
    cheese, divided
¼ cup frozen egg substitute, thawed
2 tablespoons skim milk
1½ tablespoons chopped fresh basil
¼ teaspoon salt
¼ teaspoon pepper
⅓ cup all-purpose flour
1¾ cups skim milk
⅓ cup dry white wine
½ pound fresh lump crabmeat, drained
6 lasagna noodles (cooked without salt or fat)
¼ cup freshly grated Parmesan cheese
½ teaspoon paprika
3 cooked shrimp with tails (optional)

Drain spinach, and press dry between layers of
paper towels; set aside.

Bring water to a boil; add 1¼ pounds shrimp, and
cook 3 to 5 minutes or until shrimp turn pink. Drain;
rinse with cold water. Peel and devein shrimp.

Coat a medium saucepan with cooking spray;
place over medium-high heat until hot. Add onion,
green pepper, and garlic; sauté until tender. Transfer to a bowl. Wipe saucepan dry.

Add Neufchâtel cheese to saucepan, and cook
over medium heat, stirring constantly, until cheese
melts. Add melted Neufchâtel cheese, cottage
cheese, ½ cup Swiss cheese, and next 5 ingredients
to onion mixture; stir well. Set aside.

Place flour in a saucepan. Stir in 1¾ cups milk.
Cook over medium heat, stirring constantly, 5 minutes or until thickened. Remove from heat; stir in
peeled cooked shrimp, wine, and crabmeat.

Coat a 13- x 9- x 2-inch baking dish with cooking
spray. Place 3 lasagna noodles in bottom of dish.
Top with half of cottage cheese mixture, half of
spinach, and half of seafood mixture. Repeat layers.

Combine remaining ¼ cup Swiss cheese,
Parmesan cheese, and paprika; sprinkle over
lasagna. Cover and bake at 350° for 40 minutes.
Uncover and bake an additional 10 minutes. Let
lasagna stand 10 minutes before serving. Garnish
with 3 cooked shrimp with tails, if desired. Yield:
8 servings.

PER SERVING: 355 CALORIES (30% FROM FAT)
FAT 11.7G (SATURATED FAT 6.5G)
PROTEIN 36.1G CARBOHYDRATE 26.2G
CHOLESTEROL 138MG   SODIUM 750MG

LEMON SQUASH

This recipe can be made in about 15 minutes.

2¼ cups diagonally sliced yellow squash
2¼ cups diagonally sliced zucchini
¼ cup canned no-salt-added chicken broth,
    undiluted
1 tablespoon lemon juice
1 teaspoon cornstarch
2 teaspoons reduced-calorie margarine
¼ teaspoon dried oregano
¼ teaspoon salt
¼ teaspoon pepper
Fresh oregano sprigs (optional)

Arrange squash and zucchini in a steamer basket
over boiling water. Cover and steam 6 minutes or
until crisp-tender; place in a serving bowl.

Combine chicken broth and next 6 ingredients
in a small saucepan, stirring until smooth. Cook
over medium heat, stirring constantly, until slightly
thickened. Pour mixture over vegetables; toss
gently. Garnish with oregano sprigs, if desired.
Yield: 8 (½-cup) servings.

PER SERVING: 18 CALORIES (35% FROM FAT)
FAT 0.7G (SATURATED FAT 0.1G)
PROTEIN 0.7G CARBOHYDRATE 2.9G
CHOLESTEROL 0MG   SODIUM 84MG

MIXED GREENS WITH WALNUT VINAIGRETTE

2 cups torn curly endive
2 cups loosely packed watercress leaves
2 cups torn fresh spinach
2 cups torn red leaf lettuce
½ cup sliced water chestnuts
½ cup julienne-sliced sweet red pepper
⅓ cup rice wine vinegar
1 tablespoon chopped fresh chives
1 tablespoon water
2 teaspoons walnut oil
1 teaspoon white wine Worcestershire sauce
½ teaspoon sugar
⅛ teaspoon salt
⅛ teaspoon pepper
2½ tablespoons finely chopped walnuts, toasted

Combine first 6 ingredients in a large bowl; toss well, and set aside.

Combine vinegar and next 7 ingredients in a small bowl, stirring well with a wire whisk. Stir in walnuts; pour over lettuce mixture, and toss gently. Yield: 8 (1-cup) servings.

PER SERVING: 41 CALORIES (61% FROM FAT)
FAT 2.8G (SATURATED FAT 0.2G)
PROTEIN 1.4G   CARBOHYDRATE 3.1G
CHOLESTEROL 0MG   SODIUM 55MG

ORANGE MARMALADE TEA CAKES

¼ cup margarine, softened
1½ ounces Neufchâtel cheese, softened
2 tablespoons frozen egg substitute, thawed
1 teaspoon vanilla extract
⅔ cup all-purpose flour
½ teaspoon baking powder
3 tablespoons sugar
¼ cup low-sugar orange marmalade
Vegetable cooking spray
½ cup sifted powdered sugar
2 teaspoons unsweetened orange juice

Combine margarine and Neufchâtel cheese in a bowl; beat at medium speed of an electric mixer until creamy. Add egg substitute and vanilla, beating well.

Combine flour, baking powder, and 3 tablespoons sugar; add to margarine mixture, beating well. Stir in marmalade.

Drop dough by level tablespoonfuls, 2 inches apart, onto cookie sheets coated with cooking spray. Bake at 350° for 10 to 12 minutes or until edges are golden. Remove from cookie sheets, and let cool completely on wire racks.

Combine powdered sugar and orange juice, stirring until smooth. Spread over cooled cookies. Yield: 1½ dozen.

PER COOKIE: 70 CALORIES (41% FROM FAT)
FAT 3.2G (SATURATED FAT 0.9G)
PROTEIN 0.9G   CARBOHYDRATE 9.4G
CHOLESTEROL 2MG   SODIUM 42MG

MOCHA CAPPUCCINO

For a nonalcoholic beverage, omit the Frangelico and increase the chocolate syrup to ½ cup.

5½ cups warm brewed coffee
¼ cup plus 2 tablespoons chocolate syrup
2 tablespoons Frangelico or other hazelnut-flavored liqueur
½ cup frozen reduced-calorie whipped topping, thawed
1 tablespoon plus 1 teaspoon grated semisweet chocolate

Combine coffee, chocolate syrup, and liqueur, stirring well. Pour evenly into serving mugs. Top each serving with 1 tablespoon whipped topping and ½ teaspoon grated chocolate. Serve immediately. Yield: 8 (¾-cup) servings.

PER SERVING: 69 CALORIES (17% FROM FAT)
FAT 1.3G (SATURATED FAT 0.7G)
PROTEIN 0.8G   CARBOHYDRATE 12.1G
CHOLESTEROL 0MG   SODIUM 16MG

Southern-Style Bouillabaisse (recipe on page 41)

APPETIZERS & SOUPS

*L*obster bisque, New Orleans-style gumbo, clam chowder. No, you're not reading the menu of some exclusive restaurant. You are simply getting a sampling of the treats awaiting you as you turn the pages of this chapter. As a bonus, you can enjoy these specialties and still keep your fat budget under control.

Before you get to the bisques and chowders, look for Tuna Niçoise Canapés (page 30) and Appetizer Clams with Mango Salsa (page 33). Either would be a great starter for an elegant dinner party. And no seafood cookbook is complete without cocktail sauce—the one on page 39 has a southwestern twist. Serve it with chilled shrimp as an appetizer or a light supper entrée.

SALMON WITH FRESH ASPARAGUS

16 fresh asparagus spears
1 (8-ounce) package nonfat cream cheese, softened
1 tablespoon skim milk
1 tablespoon chopped fresh dill
1 tablespoon capers
16 (⅛-inch-thick) slices smoked salmon (about 12 ounces)
Fresh dill sprigs (optional)

Snap off tough ends of asparagus. Remove scales from stalks with a knife or vegetable peeler, if desired. Cut asparagus in half crosswise. Reserve asparagus bottoms for another use. Arrange asparagus in a steamer basket over boiling water. Cover and steam 1 minute or until crisp-tender. Rinse with cold water; drain well, and set aside.

Combine cream cheese and milk, stirring until smooth. Stir in chopped dill and capers. Spread cream cheese mixture evenly over one side of each salmon slice. Place 1 asparagus piece across narrow end of each slice. Roll up slices, jellyroll fashion.

Place salmon rolls on a serving platter. Cover and chill thoroughly. Garnish with dill sprigs, if desired. Yield: 16 appetizers.

PER APPETIZER: 39 CALORIES (21% FROM FAT)
FAT 0.9G (SATURATED FAT 0.2G)
PROTEIN 6.1G   CARBOHYDRATE 0.9G
CHOLESTEROL 7MG   SODIUM 309MG

SMOKED SALMON SPREAD

¾ pound smoked salmon, cut into 1-inch pieces
½ cup chopped green onions
1 tablespoon Dijon mustard
1 teaspoon lemon juice
½ teaspoon ground white pepper
1 cup plain nonfat yogurt
2 hard-cooked egg whites, diced
3 tablespoons minced fresh chives

Position knife blade in food processor bowl. Add first 5 ingredients. Pulse 8 times or until mixture is minced. Place mixture on a sheet of heavy-duty plastic wrap, and shape into a 2-inch-thick patty. Cover and chill at least 8 hours.

Spoon yogurt onto several layers of heavy-duty paper towels; spread to ½-inch thickness. Cover with additional paper towels; let stand 5 minutes. Scrape into a bowl, using a rubber spatula; cover and chill thoroughly.

Place salmon patty on a serving platter; spread yogurt over top and sides of patty. Sprinkle diced egg white and chives over yogurt. Serve with cucumber slices or Melba rounds. Yield: 1¾ cups.

PER TABLESPOON: 22 CALORIES (25% FROM FAT)
FAT 0.6G (SATURATED FAT 0.1G)
PROTEIN 3.0G   CARBOHYDRATE 0.9G
CHOLESTEROL 3MG   SODIUM 122MG

TUNA NIÇOISE CANAPÉS

24 (¼-inch-thick) slices baking potato (about 2 medium)
Vegetable cooking spray
2 tablespoons malt vinegar
1 teaspoon dried thyme, divided
¼ teaspoon garlic powder
⅛ teaspoon salt
¾ cup thinly sliced fresh green beans
½ teaspoon freshly ground pepper
1 (5-ounce) tuna steak (¾ inch thick)
2 teaspoons olive oil, divided
2½ tablespoons nonfat sour cream
1 tablespoon Dijon mustard
2 teaspoons capers
12 cherry tomatoes

Arrange potato slices in a single layer on a baking sheet coated with cooking spray. Spray slices with cooking spray. Turn slices, and spray again; brush with vinegar. Combine ½ teaspoon thyme, garlic powder, and salt; sprinkle evenly over slices. Bake at 400° for 15 minutes or until tender; let cool.

Arrange beans in a steamer basket over boiling water. Cover; steam 10 minutes or until tender.

Press pepper into both sides of tuna. Coat a

nonstick skillet with cooking spray; add 1 teaspoon oil. Place over medium-high heat until hot. Add tuna; cook 4 minutes on each side or until fish flakes easily when tested with a fork. Remove from heat; let cool completely.

Flake tuna; place in a bowl. Add beans; toss well. Combine remaining ½ teaspoon thyme, remaining 1 teaspoon oil, sour cream, mustard, and capers; add to tuna mixture, and stir well.

Arrange potato slices on a serving platter. Cut each cherry tomato into 4 slices; arrange 2 tomato slices on top of each potato slice. Spoon tuna mixture over tomato slices. Yield: 24 appetizers.

PER APPETIZER: 34 CALORIES (24% FROM FAT)
FAT 0.9G (SATURATED FAT 0.2G)
PROTEIN 2.1G   CARBOHYDRATE 4.4G
CHOLESTEROL 2MG   SODIUM 52MG

Tuna Niçoise Canapés

STUFFED CHILE BITES

3 ounces Neufchâtel cheese, softened
2 tablespoons nonfat mayonnaise-type salad
   dressing
1 (6⅛-ounce) can 60% less-salt tuna in water,
   drained
1 (2-ounce) can chopped green chiles, drained
2 tablespoons finely chopped green onions
2 tablespoons minced fresh cilantro
½ teaspoon ground cumin
4 mild poblano chiles (about 4 inches long),
   cored and seeded
Fresh cilantro sprigs (optional)

Combine Neufchâtel cheese and salad dressing in a medium bowl; beat at low speed of an electric mixer until smooth. Add tuna and next 4 ingredients, stirring well. Spoon tuna mixture evenly into chiles; cover and chill at least 2 hours.

To serve, cut chiles into 1-inch slices, and arrange on a serving platter. Garnish with fresh cilantro sprigs, if desired. Yield: 16 appetizers.

PER APPETIZER: 37 CALORIES (32% FROM FAT)
FAT 1.3G (SATURATED FAT 0.8G)
PROTEIN 4.1G CARBOHYDRATE 2.3G
CHOLESTEROL 9MG SODIUM 73MG

SOUTHWESTERN TUNA PÂTÉ

2 (6½-ounce) cans white tuna in water,
   drained
3 tablespoons reduced-fat mayonnaise
¼ cup minced fresh chives
¼ cup minced fresh cilantro
2 tablespoons lime juice
2 tablespoons tequila
¼ teaspoon dried crushed red pepper
Fresh cilantro sprigs (optional)
Jalapeño pepper slices (optional)

Combine tuna and mayonnaise in a small bowl; stir well. Add chives, cilantro, lime juice, tequila, and crushed red pepper. Transfer mixture to a small crock or bowl. Cover and chill at least 1 hour. If desired, garnish with fresh cilantro sprigs and jalapeño pepper slices. Serve pâté with cucumber slices or melba rounds. Yield: 1½ cups.

PER TABLESPOON: 23 CALORIES (31% FROM FAT)
FAT 0.8G (SATURATED FAT 0.1G)
PROTEIN 2.9G CARBOHYDRATE 0.3G
CHOLESTEROL 5MG SODIUM 56MG

STONE CRAB CLAWS WITH FENNEL AÏOLI

Aïoli is a garlic-flavored condiment that originated in southern France.

¾ pound fennel
Vegetable cooking spray
2 tablespoons dry white wine
4 large cloves garlic, sliced
1 cup 1% low-fat cottage cheese
½ cup plain nonfat yogurt
3 tablespoons Dijon mustard
1 teaspoon lemon juice
½ teaspoon ground red pepper
24 (3-ounce) precooked stone crab claws,
   chilled

Trim off leaves of fennel, reserving for other uses. Trim off tough outer stalks, and discard. Cut bulb in half lengthwise; remove and discard core. Cut bulb crosswise into ⅛-inch slices.

Coat a medium nonstick skillet with cooking spray; place over medium-high heat until hot. Add fennel, wine, and garlic; sauté until tender. Remove from heat, and let cool.

Combine fennel mixture, cottage cheese, yogurt, mustard, lemon juice, and red pepper in container of an electric blender or food processor; cover and process until smooth. Cover mixture, and chill at least 1 hour. Serve aïoli with stone crab claws. Yield: 24 appetizers.

PER APPETIZER: 37 CALORIES (17% FROM FAT)
FAT 0.7G (SATURATED FAT 0.1G)
PROTEIN 6.0G CARBOHYDRATE 1.4G
CHOLESTEROL 22MG SODIUM 158MG

Appetizer Clams with Mango Salsa

APPETIZER CLAMS WITH MANGO SALSA

1 cup peeled, diced fresh ripe mango
1 cup seeded, diced unpeeled tomato
3 tablespoons finely chopped purple onion
2 tablespoons fresh lime juice
¼ teaspoon salt
⅛ teaspoon dried crushed red pepper
48 small clams in shells, scrubbed
2 tablespoons cornmeal

Combine first 6 ingredients in a bowl; stir gently. Cover and chill salsa.

Place clams in a large bowl, and cover with cold water. Sprinkle with cornmeal, and let stand 30 minutes. Drain and rinse; discard cornmeal. Place a mesh rack on a grill rack over hot coals. Place clams on mesh rack; cook 10 to 15 minutes or until shells open. Discard any unopened shells. Divide clams among 8 individual serving bowls; add ¼ cup salsa to each. Yield: 8 appetizer servings.

PER SERVING: 99 CALORIES (11% FROM FAT)
FAT 1.2G (SATURATED FAT 0.1G)
PROTEIN 13.9G   CARBOHYDRATE 8.0G
CHOLESTEROL 36MG   SODIUM 135MG

Hot Spinach-Crabmeat Dip

HOT SPINACH-CRABMEAT DIP

¾ cup nonfat ricotta cheese
¾ cup plus 2 tablespoons skim milk
½ cup nonfat mayonnaise
1 tablespoon dry sherry
1 (10-ounce) package frozen chopped spinach, thawed
1 (8-ounce) can sliced water chestnuts, drained and chopped
6 ounces fresh lump crabmeat, drained
¾ cup (3 ounces) shredded reduced-fat Monterey Jack cheese
½ cup drained, finely diced roasted red pepper in water
¼ cup minced green onions
½ teaspoon hot sauce
Vegetable cooking spray

Press ricotta cheese through a fine-mesh sieve into a large bowl. Add skim milk, mayonnaise, and sherry; stir well.

Drain spinach; press between paper towels to remove excess moisture. Add spinach, water chestnuts, and next 5 ingredients to cheese mixture; stir well. Spoon mixture into a 1½-quart baking dish coated with cooking spray. Cover and bake at 350° for 30 minutes. Uncover and bake 10 additional minutes or until hot and bubbly. Serve with toasted pita wedges. Yield: 4¾ cups.

PER TABLESPOON: 12 CALORIES (23% FROM FAT)
FAT 0.3G (SATURATED FAT 0.1G)
PROTEIN 1.4G   CARBOHYDRATE 1.1G
CHOLESTEROL 3MG   SODIUM 62MG

LOUISIANA CRAB CAKES

These crab cakes can be served with fat-free tartar sauce or low-sodium cocktail sauce.

1 pound fresh lump crabmeat, drained
1½ cups soft breadcrumbs
3 tablespoons finely chopped green onions
2 tablespoons fresh lemon juice
2 tablespoons nonfat mayonnaise
½ teaspoon paprika
⅛ teaspoon salt
1 egg white, beaten
1 jalapeño pepper, seeded and finely chopped
Vegetable cooking spray
2 teaspoons vegetable oil, divided
Lemon wedges (optional)
Fresh chives (optional)

Combine first 9 ingredients in a medium bowl, stirring well. Shape mixture into 8 (½-inch-thick) patties.

Coat a large nonstick skillet with cooking spray; add 1 teaspoon oil. Place over medium heat until hot. Place 4 patties in skillet, and cook 3 minutes on each side or until golden. Repeat procedure with remaining 1 teaspoon oil and 4 patties. If desired, garnish with lemon wedges and chives. Yield: 8 appetizers.

PER APPETIZER: 94 CALORIES (23% FROM FAT)
FAT 2.4G (SATURATED FAT 0.4G)
PROTEIN 11.9G   CARBOHYDRATE 5.6G
CHOLESTEROL 53MG   SODIUM 279MG

Buying Fresh Crabmeat

You can purchase fresh cooked crabmeat in the lump form (whole pieces of the white body meat), flaked form (small pieces of white and dark meat from the body and claws), and claw form. Before purchasing, make sure the crabmeat is moist and has no strong odor. You should serve cooked fresh crabmeat within two days of purchase. Other convenient forms of crabmeat include pasteurized (often available in containers alongside fresh seafood), canned, and frozen. These are suitable for use in some casseroles, dips, sauces, and stuffings.

Mussels in Tomato-Wine Sauce

MUSSELS IN TOMATO-WINE SAUCE

1 pound fresh mussels
2 teaspoons olive oil
1 cup chopped onion
3 cloves garlic, minced
2 (14½-ounce) cans no-salt-added whole
   tomatoes, drained and chopped
½ cup dry white wine
⅓ cup chopped fresh basil
¼ teaspoon freshly ground pepper
12 (½-inch-thick) slices French baguette,
   toasted
Fresh basil sprigs (optional)

Remove beards on mussels, and scrub shells with a brush. Discard open, cracked, or heavy mussels (they're filled with sand). Set aside remaining mussels.

Heat oil in a large saucepan over medium-high heat until hot. Add onion and garlic; sauté 4 minutes or until tender. Add tomatoes and wine; bring to a boil. Add mussels, basil, and pepper. Cover, reduce heat to medium-low, and simmer 3 to 5 minutes or until mussels open. Discard unopened mussels.

Spoon mussels and tomato mixture into individual serving bowls. Serve with baguette slices. Garnish with basil sprigs, if desired. Yield: 6 appetizer servings.

PER SERVING: 121 CALORIES (18% FROM FAT)
FAT 2.4G (SATURATED FAT 0.4G)
PROTEIN 6.9G   CARBOHYDRATE 18.5G
CHOLESTEROL 9MG   SODIUM 196MG

THAI BARBECUED OYSTERS

Rock salt
12 fresh oysters (in the shell)
2 tablespoons low-sodium barbecue sauce
¼ cup fine, dry breadcrumbs
¼ cup minced fresh cilantro
3 tablespoons minced green onions
1 tablespoon peeled, grated gingerroot

Sprinkle a layer of rock salt in a 15- x 10- x 1-inch jellyroll pan; set pan aside.

Scrub oyster shells, and open, discarding top shells. Arrange half shells with oysters over rock salt. Brush oysters with barbecue sauce.

Combine breadcrumbs and remaining 3 ingredients in a small bowl; stir well. Sprinkle evenly over oysters. Bake at 425° for 12 minutes or until oysters begin to curl. Yield: 12 appetizers.

Note: Shucked fresh oysters sold in plastic tubs may be substituted for oysters in shells. Prepare recipe in shell-shaped baking dishes.

PER APPETIZER: 30 CALORIES (24% FROM FAT)
FAT 0.8G (SATURATED FAT 0.2G)
PROTEIN 2.2G   CARBOHYDRATE 2.7G
CHOLESTEROL 15MG   SODIUM 70MG

Attached to the shells of fresh mussels are strands of tissue called "beards" that you should remove before cooking. Mussels spoil very quickly after debearding, so prepare them immediately.

TOMATILLO SALSA-SCALLOP APPETIZERS

⅔ cup husked, diced tomatillos
⅔ cup diced jicama
½ cup minced green onions
½ cup lime juice
⅓ cup minced fresh cilantro
¼ teaspoon salt
¼ teaspoon garlic powder
Vegetable cooking spray
1½ teaspoons olive oil
½ cup minced shallots
1 pound bay scallops
½ cup crushed ice
6 large Bibb lettuce leaves
3 medium tomatoes, each cut into 4 slices

Combine first 7 ingredients in a medium bowl. Cover and chill 1 hour.

Coat a large nonstick skillet with cooking spray; add oil. Place over medium-high heat until hot. Add shallots; sauté 2 minutes or until tender. Add scallops, and sauté 2 minutes or until scallops are opaque.

Add crushed ice to tomatillo mixture. Immediately add scallop mixture to tomatillo mixture; stir well. Cover and chill at least 2 hours.

To serve, arrange a lettuce leaf and 2 tomato slices on each individual serving plate. Spoon scallop mixture evenly onto tomato, using a slotted spoon. Yield: 6 appetizer servings.

PER SERVING: 120 CALORIES (17% FROM FAT)
FAT 2.2G (SATURATED FAT 0.3G)
PROTEIN 14.3G   CARBOHYDRATE 11.8G
CHOLESTEROL 25MG   SODIUM 233MG

Southwestern Cocktail Sauce

SOUTHWESTERN COCKTAIL SAUCE

1 (8-ounce) can no-salt-added tomato sauce
¼ cup chopped fresh cilantro
1 tablespoon finely chopped onion
1½ tablespoons lime juice
1 tablespoon prepared horseradish
1 jalapeño pepper, seeded and chopped
½ teaspoon garlic powder
½ teaspoon onion powder
½ teaspoon salt
⅛ teaspoon hot sauce
Fresh jalapeño pepper (optional)

Combine first 10 ingredients in a bowl; stir well. Cover and chill 3 hours. Transfer to a serving bowl; garnish with jalapeño pepper, if desired. Serve with cooked shrimp or other shellfish. Yield: 1 cup.

PER TABLESPOON: 7 CALORIES (0% FROM FAT)
FAT 0.0G (SATURATED FAT 0.0G)
PROTEIN 0.2G CARBOHYDRATE 1.6G
CHOLESTEROL 0MG SODIUM 42MG

BAKED STUFFED SHRIMP

1 (8-ounce) package fresh, washed and
    trimmed spinach
Vegetable cooking spray
½ teaspoon olive oil
1 cup finely chopped fresh mushrooms
¼ cup minced shallots
¼ cup plus 2 tablespoons freshly grated
    Parmesan cheese, divided
2 tablespoons minced fresh basil
½ teaspoon hot sauce
16 unpeeled jumbo fresh shrimp
1 tablespoon fresh lemon juice

Cook spinach in a small amount of boiling water 1 minute. Drain well; chop spinach, and set aside.

Coat a large nonstick skillet with cooking spray; add oil. Place over medium-high heat until hot. Add mushrooms and shallots; sauté 5 minutes. Add spinach; cook over medium heat 5 minutes, stirring frequently. Remove from heat; stir in ¼ cup Parmesan cheese, basil, and hot sauce. Set aside.

Peel and devein shrimp, leaving tails intact. Butterfly shrimp; brush with lemon juice. Top each with 1 tablespoon plus 1 teaspoon spinach mixture.

Place shrimp on a baking sheet coated with cooking spray. Sprinkle remaining 2 tablespoons cheese over spinach mixture. Bake at 350° for 14 minutes or until shrimp turn pink. Yield: 16 appetizers.

PER APPETIZER: 41 CALORIES (29% FROM FAT)
FAT 1.3G (SATURATED FAT 0.5G)
PROTEIN 5.8G CARBOHYDRATE 1.5G
CHOLESTEROL 34MG SODIUM 87MG

SHRIMP EN PAPILLOTE

1 (8-ounce) can unsweetened pineapple chunks
2 tablespoons honey
2 tablespoons fresh lemon juice
1 tablespoon low-sodium soy sauce
1 tablespoon red wine vinegar
1 teaspoon cornstarch
1 teaspoon peeled, minced gingerroot
2 cups sliced fresh mushrooms
¼ cup thinly sliced green onions
24 unpeeled medium-size fresh shrimp

Drain pineapple, reserving juice; set pineapple aside. Combine pineapple juice, honey, and next 5 ingredients in a bowl; stir well. Combine mushrooms and green onions in a small bowl; toss well.

Peel and devein shrimp. Cut 8 (15-inch) squares of parchment paper. Fold each square in half; open each, and divide pineapple chunks and shrimp among squares, near fold. Top each with ¼ cup mushroom mixture. Drizzle 1 teaspoon pineapple juice mixture over each serving; discard remaining mixture.

Fold paper, and seal edges with narrow folds; place packets on baking sheets. Bake at 400° for 10 minutes or until puffed and lightly browned. Place packets on individual serving plates, and cut open. Yield: 8 appetizer servings.

PER SERVING: 118 CALORIES (12% FROM FAT)
FAT 1.6G (SATURATED FAT 0.3G)
PROTEIN 17.7G CARBOHYDRATE 7.5G
CHOLESTEROL 129MG SODIUM 140MG

Vegetable Bisque with Seafood

VEGETABLE BISQUE WITH SEAFOOD

3 cups frozen whole-kernel corn, thawed and
    divided
2 cups low-sodium chicken broth, divided
¾ pound unpeeled medium-size fresh shrimp
1 tablespoon olive oil
1 cup chopped onion
1 cup chopped green pepper
1 cup chopped sweet red pepper
1 cup skim milk
¼ cup chopped fresh cilantro
¼ cup chopped fresh parsley
¼ teaspoon salt
⅛ teaspoon pepper

   Combine 2 cups corn and 1 cup broth in container of an electric blender; cover and process
until smooth. Set pureed corn mixture aside.
   Peel and devein shrimp; set aside.
   Heat oil in a large saucepan over medium heat.
Add onion, green pepper, and red pepper; sauté 5
minutes or until tender. Stir in pureed corn mixture, remaining 1 cup broth, and milk; bring to a
boil. Cover, reduce heat, and simmer 5 minutes.
   Add remaining 1 cup corn, shrimp, cilantro, and
remaining 3 ingredients; cover and simmer 5 minutes or until shrimp turn pink. Yield: 7 (1-cup)
servings.

PER SERVING: 174 CALORIES (21% FROM FAT)
FAT 4.1G (SATURATED FAT 0.7G)
PROTEIN 14.6G CARBOHYDRATE 22.1G
CHOLESTEROL 75MG   SODIUM 203MG

LOBSTER BISQUE

Making a quick stock from a lobster shell gives this soup its great taste.

1 (1¼-pound) lobster, cooked
1¼ cups water
1 (8-ounce) bottle clam juice
2 whole cloves
1 bay leaf
2 teaspoons margarine
Vegetable cooking spray
¼ cup finely chopped onion
¼ cup finely chopped celery
¼ cup all-purpose flour
2 cups 2% low-fat milk
2½ tablespoons tomato paste
¼ teaspoon salt
Dash of ground red pepper
1 tablespoon dry sherry
Celery leaves (optional)

Remove meat from cooked lobster tail and claws; chop meat, and set aside. Place lobster shell in a large heavy-duty, zip-top plastic bag. Coarsely crush shell, using a meat mallet or rolling pin. Place crushed shell in a large saucepan; add water and next 3 ingredients. Partially cover, and cook over medium-low heat 30 minutes. Strain shell mixture through a sieve, reserving stock. Discard shell pieces, cloves, and bay leaf.

Melt margarine in a large saucepan coated with cooking spray over medium heat. Add onion and celery; sauté 3 minutes. Sprinkle onion mixture with flour; stir well, and cook, stirring constantly, 1 minute.

Gradually add reserved lobster stock, milk, tomato paste, salt, and red pepper; cook over medium heat, stirring constantly, 8 minutes or until thickened. Stir in chopped lobster meat, and cook, stirring constantly, 1 additional minute. Remove from heat, and stir in sherry. Garnish with celery leaves, if desired. Yield: 4 (1-cup) servings.

PER SERVING: 152 CALORIES (29% FROM FAT)
FAT 4.9G (SATURATED FAT 1.9G)
PROTEIN 11.0G   CARBOHYDRATE 15.5G
CHOLESTEROL 37MG   SODIUM 367MG

SOUTHERN-STYLE BOUILLABAISSE

(pictured on page 28)

You may use sea scallops instead of bay, if you prefer. Just cut them in half before adding to the bouillabaisse.

Olive oil-flavored vegetable cooking spray
1 large onion, chopped
1 stalk celery, chopped
¾ cup thinly sliced leeks
3 cloves garlic, minced
3 (14½-ounce) cans no-salt-added whole tomatoes, undrained and chopped
1 cup dry white wine
1 cup water
¾ cup clam juice
½ (10-ounce) package frozen cut okra, thawed
2 tablespoons chopped fresh parsley
¾ teaspoon dried Italian seasoning
½ teaspoon dried basil
¼ teaspoon powdered saffron
1 bay leaf
¾ pound unpeeled medium-size fresh shrimp
¾ pound orange roughy or other white fish fillets, cut into 1½-inch pieces
½ pound fresh bay scallops

Coat a Dutch oven with cooking spray; add onion, celery, leeks, and garlic. Sauté 5 minutes or until vegetables are tender.

Add tomatoes and next 9 ingredients. Bring to a boil over medium-high heat. Cover, reduce heat, and simmer 20 minutes.

Peel and devein shrimp. Add shrimp, fish, and scallops to tomato mixture, stirring well; cook 5 minutes over medium-high heat or until shrimp turn pink and fish flakes easily when tested with a fork. Remove and discard bay leaf. Yield: 12 servings.

PER SERVING: 95 CALORIES (9% FROM FAT)
FAT 0.9G (SATURATED FAT 0.1G)
PROTEIN 13.1G   CARBOHYDRATE 8.8G
CHOLESTEROL 44MG   SODIUM 132MG

New England Fish Chowder

4 cups water
1 pound cod or other white fish fillets
2 tablespoons margarine
3 tablespoons shredded carrot
2 tablespoons diced celery
2 tablespoons minced fresh onion
2 tablespoons plus 1 teaspoon all-purpose flour
3½ cups skim milk, divided
2 cups peeled, diced baking potato
¼ teaspoon salt
¼ teaspoon pepper
Unsalted oyster crackers (optional)

Bring water to a boil in a large skillet. Add fish; cover, reduce heat, and simmer 7 minutes or until fish flakes easily when tested with a fork. Remove fish from skillet with a slotted spatula; set aside.

Melt margarine in a saucepan over medium heat. Add carrot, celery, and onion; sauté 2 minutes. Stir in flour. Gradually add 2½ cups milk, stirring constantly with a wire whisk. Add potato, salt, and pepper; reduce heat, and cook, uncovered, 30 minutes, stirring occasionally. Add fish and remaining 1 cup milk; cook 10 additional minutes or until thoroughly heated. Serve with unsalted oyster crackers, if desired. Yield: 4 (1½-cup) servings.

PER SERVING: 300 CALORIES (21% FROM FAT)
FAT 7.0G (SATURATED FAT 1.6G)
PROTEIN 29.7G   CARBOHYDRATE 28.6G
CHOLESTEROL 53MG   SODIUM 396MG

New England Fish Chowder

HARVEST CLAM CHOWDER

Instead of cream, this hearty chowder calls for a combination of low-fat milk and a rich-tasting vegetable puree as its base.

2¼ cups peeled, cubed baking potato
2½ cups canned low-sodium chicken broth, undiluted and divided
1 cup chopped onion
¾ cup chopped celery
½ cup finely chopped sweet red pepper
¼ cup finely chopped carrot
1⅓ cups 1% low-fat milk
1 (10-ounce) can whole baby clams, undrained
¼ cup chopped fresh parsley
½ teaspoon hot sauce
¼ teaspoon coarsely ground pepper

Combine potato and 1½ cups broth in a Dutch oven; bring to a boil. Reduce heat, and simmer, uncovered, 10 to 12 minutes or until potato is tender. Remove half of potato from liquid, using a slotted spoon; set aside. Pour remaining potato mixture into container of an electric blender. Cover and process until smooth; set aside.

Place ½ cup of remaining chicken broth, onion, and next 3 ingredients in Dutch oven. Bring to a boil; reduce heat, and simmer, uncovered, 10 to 15 minutes or until liquid evaporates. Add 1 cup vegetable mixture to potato puree in blender; cover and process until smooth, stopping once to scrape down sides.

Add reserved cubed potato, pureed potato mixture, remaining ½ cup broth, and milk to vegetable mixture in Dutch oven. Bring to a boil; reduce heat, and simmer, uncovered, 8 minutes.

Drain clams, reserving liquid. Add clam liquid, parsley, hot sauce, and pepper to Dutch oven; stir well. Cook, uncovered, 5 minutes. Add clams, and cook 2 additional minutes. Ladle soup into individual bowls. Yield: 6 (1-cup) servings.

PER SERVING: 126 CALORIES (12% FROM FAT)
FAT 1.7G (SATURATED FAT 0.7G)
PROTEIN 8.3G   CARBOHYDRATE 19.8G
CHOLESTEROL 17MG   SODIUM 352MG

OYSTER AND CORN CHOWDER

A trip to the Chesapeake would be incomplete without a bowl of oyster chowder.

2 (12-ounce) containers standard oysters, undrained
¼ cup all-purpose flour
1 tablespoon margarine
½ cup chopped onion
⅓ cup chopped celery
⅓ cup chopped carrot
4 cups 2% low-fat milk
2 cups diced red potato
1 (16-ounce) package frozen whole-kernel corn
1 teaspoon salt
½ teaspoon hot sauce
⅛ teaspoon pepper
¼ cup plus 3 tablespoons chopped green onions

Drain oysters, reserving liquor, and set oysters aside. Place flour in a small bowl. Gradually add oyster liquor, stirring with a wire whisk until blended; set aside.

Melt margarine in a Dutch oven over medium heat. Add onion, celery, and carrot; sauté 5 minutes. Add milk and diced potato; bring to a simmer. Cover and cook 10 minutes. Add corn; cover and cook 5 minutes. Add oysters, oyster liquor mixture, salt, hot sauce, and pepper; cook, uncovered, 6 minutes or until edges of oysters curl. Ladle into soup bowls, and top with green onions. Yield: 7 (1½-cup) servings.

PER SERVING: 244 CALORIES (23% FROM FAT)
FAT 6.2G (SATURATED FAT 2.5G)
PROTEIN 13.1G   CARBOHYDRATE 36.1G
CHOLESTEROL 49MG   SODIUM 517MG

SEAFOOD GUMBO

1 pound unpeeled medium-size fresh shrimp
⅓ cup all-purpose flour
Vegetable cooking spray
2 teaspoons vegetable oil
1½ cups chopped onion
1 cup chopped sweet yellow pepper
½ cup chopped celery
1 tablespoon chopped garlic
2⅓ cups sliced fresh okra (about ⅔ pound)
⅓ cup no-salt-added tomato paste
2 cups water
2 (14½-ounce) cans no-salt-added whole
   tomatoes, undrained and chopped
2 (10½-ounce) cans low-sodium chicken broth
1 teaspoon dried thyme
½ teaspoon ground red pepper
½ teaspoon salt
½ pound fresh lump crabmeat, drained
½ cup diced turkey ham
½ cup chopped fresh parsley
2 teaspoons hot sauce

Peel and devein shrimp; set aside.

Place flour in a small nonstick skillet. Cook over medium-high heat 8 to 10 minutes or until lightly browned, stirring frequently; set aside.

Coat a Dutch oven with cooking spray; add oil. Place over medium-high heat until hot. Add onion, chopped pepper, celery, and garlic; sauté 15 minutes. Add okra and tomato paste; cook, stirring constantly, 1 minute. Add water and next 5 ingredients; bring to a boil. Reduce heat, and simmer, uncovered, 40 minutes.

Combine browned flour and 2 cups cooking liquid from Dutch oven, stirring until smooth. Add flour mixture to Dutch oven, stirring constantly with a wire whisk. Bring to a boil. Reduce heat, and cook, uncovered, 10 minutes. Add shrimp, crabmeat, and ham; cover and cook 3 to 5 minutes or until shrimp turn pink. Stir in chopped parsley and hot sauce. Yield: 8 (1½-cup) servings.

PER SERVING: 188 CALORIES (18% FROM FAT)
FAT 3.8G (SATURATED FAT 0.8G)
PROTEIN 20.1G CARBOHYDRATE 19.1G
CHOLESTEROL 100MG SODIUM 504MG

LINGUINE-CLAM SOUP

Vegetable cooking spray
½ cup diced sweet yellow pepper
2 cloves garlic, minced
4 cups water
2 tablespoons minced fresh basil
2 teaspoons chicken-flavored bouillon granules
2 ounces linguine, uncooked and broken into
   2-inch pieces
2 cups peeled, seeded, and diced tomato
2 (6½-ounce) cans minced clams, undrained
¼ cup minced fresh parsley
¼ teaspoon cracked pepper
2 tablespoons plus 1 teaspoon grated
   Parmesan cheese

Coat a Dutch oven with cooking spray; place over medium-high heat until hot. Add yellow pepper and garlic; sauté 2 minutes. Add water, basil, and bouillon granules. Bring to a boil.

Add linguine; return to a boil, and cook 11 minutes or until linguine is tender. Add tomato, clams, parsley, and cracked pepper. Cook until thoroughly heated. Ladle soup into individual bowls, and sprinkle each serving with 1 teaspoon Parmesan cheese. Yield: 7 (1-cup) servings.

PER SERVING: 85 CALORIES (17% FROM FAT)
FAT 1.6G (SATURATED FAT 0.6G)
PROTEIN 6.7G CARBOHYDRATE 11.3G
CHOLESTEROL 18MG SODIUM 572MG

FYI

The word "gumbo" comes from an African word for okra—a vegetable that adds both flavor and heartiness to this traditional New Orleans dish.

Another necessity for gumbo is a good roux. Typically, a roux is made by cooking flour in fat until the flour browns. The darkened roux thickens the gumbo and adds a rich taste. To eliminate unwanted fat, cook flour in a nonstick skillet without oil until the flour is browned.

FISH AND OKRA STEW

Vegetable cooking spray
1 cup diced onion
⅔ cup diced carrot
½ cup diced green pepper
½ cup diced celery
3 (6-ounce) cans spicy-hot vegetable juice
   cocktail
½ cup water
2 medium-size sweet potatoes, peeled and
   diced
6 cups sliced fresh okra
1 cup peeled, diced tomato
1 pound red snapper fillets, cut into 1-inch
   pieces

Coat a Dutch oven with cooking spray; place over medium-high heat until hot. Add onion and next 3 ingredients; sauté until tender. Add vegetable juice cocktail, water, sweet potato, okra, and tomato. Bring to a boil; cover, reduce heat, and simmer 35 minutes or until potato is tender.

Add fish; stir gently. Cover and cook 10 minutes or until fish flakes easily when tested with a fork. Yield: 9 (1-cup) servings.

PER SERVING: 149 CALORIES (7% FROM FAT)
FAT 1.1G (SATURATED FAT 0.2G)
PROTEIN 12.9G CARBOHYDRATE 21.6G
CHOLESTEROL 19MG   SODIUM 268MG

Fish and Okra Stew

Harbor Salad (recipe on page 52)

SALADS & SANDWICHES

*C*hances are that the tuna salad you remember contained quite a bit of extra fat from regular mayonnaise. But now you can bring your favorite seafood salads up to date. For starters, prepare Tuna Pasta Salad (page 50) or Shrimp Salad in Pineapple Boats (page 55).

To venture into exciting new flavors try recipes such as Grilled Halibut Salad with Raspberry Vinaigrette (page 48) or Chilled Lobster Salad with Basil-Lime Salsa (page 54).

Like salads, fish sandwiches of the past were too high in fat according to today's recommendations. In our recipe, the fillets for Oven-Fried Catfish Sandwiches (page 59) are cooked without a drop of oil, and each sandwich contains only 17% fat. You can even prepare Creole Oyster Po' Boys the low-fat way. Turn to page 62 for the lighter version.

Grilled Halibut Salad with Raspberry Vinaigrette

¼ teaspoon paprika
⅛ teaspoon freshly ground pepper
4 (6-ounce) halibut fillets
Vegetable cooking spray
¼ cup raspberry-flavored vinegar
1 tablespoon finely chopped fresh parsley
1 tablespoon extra-virgin olive oil
2 teaspoons finely chopped fresh basil
¼ teaspoon sugar
¼ teaspoon salt
8 cups gourmet salad greens

Sprinkle paprika and pepper over each side of fillets. Arrange fillets in a wire grilling basket coated with cooking spray. Place on grill rack over medium-hot coals (350° to 400°); grill, uncovered, 6 minutes on each side or until fish flakes easily when tested with a fork.

Combine vinegar and next 5 ingredients in a jar. Cover tightly, and shake vigorously. Pour over greens; toss gently. Place 2 cups greens on each of 4 plates. Cut each fillet into ¼-inch slices; arrange fillets on top of greens. Serve immediately. Yield: 4 servings.

Per Serving: 237 Calories (29% from Fat)
Fat 7.7g (Saturated Fat 1.0g)
Protein 36.9g Carbohydrate 3.0g
Cholesterol 80mg Sodium 246mg

Poached Salmon with Yellow Tomato Salsa

½ cup water
⅓ cup dry white wine
1 tablespoon coarsely chopped onion
½ teaspoon freshly ground pepper
4 (4-ounce) salmon fillets
1 cup peeled, seeded, and chopped yellow tomato
½ cup plus 2 tablespoons peeled, seeded, and chopped cucumber
⅓ cup chopped sweet red pepper
¼ cup chopped green onions
2 tablespoons chopped fresh parsley
3 tablespoons lime juice
1 teaspoon minced garlic
½ teaspoon hot sauce
¼ teaspoon salt
4 cups fresh watercress sprigs or torn leaf lettuce
Lemon wedges (optional)

Combine first 4 ingredients in a large nonstick skillet. Bring to a boil over medium heat. Reduce heat; add salmon fillets, skin side down. Cover and simmer 5 to 7 minutes or until fish flakes easily when tested with a fork. Transfer fillets and cooking liquid to a shallow baking dish. Cover and chill thoroughly.

Combine tomato and next 8 ingredients, stirring well. Cover and chill at least 1 hour.

Remove fillets from liquid; discard liquid.

Place 1 cup watercress on each of 4 individual serving plates; top with fillets. Spoon tomato mixture evenly over fillets. Garnish with lemon wedges, if desired. Yield: 4 servings.

Per Serving: 213 Calories (41% from Fat)
Fat 9.7g (Saturated Fat 1.7g)
Protein 25.0g Carbohydrate 6.5g
Cholesterol 74mg Sodium 229mg

Poached Salmon with Yellow Tomato Salsa

SCANDINAVIAN POTATO-SALMON SALAD

2 tablespoons minced fresh dill
3 tablespoons canned low-sodium chicken
    broth, undiluted
1 tablespoon white wine vinegar
1 tablespoon lemon juice
2 teaspoons olive oil
2 teaspoons Dijon mustard
¼ teaspoon salt
¼ teaspoon ground white pepper
¼ pound fresh green beans
¾ pound small round red potatoes
1 (12-ounce) salmon fillet
1 tablespoon capers
10 Boston lettuce leaves
¼ cup plus 1 tablespoon nonfat sour cream

Combine first 8 ingredients in a small bowl, stirring well with a wire whisk; set aside.

Wash beans; trim ends, and remove strings. Arrange beans in a steamer basket over boiling water. Cover and steam 4 to 6 minutes or until crisp-tender; cut into ½-inch pieces. Place in a large bowl; set aside.

Cook potatoes in a medium saucepan in boiling water to cover 15 to 17 minutes or just until tender. Remove potatoes from water, using a slotted spoon; reserve water in pan. Cut potatoes into ¼-inch-thick slices. Cut slices in half; add to beans.

Bring water in saucepan to a boil; add fillet. Cover, reduce heat, and simmer 6 to 8 minutes or until fish flakes easily when tested with a fork. Drain; remove skin from fillet. Flake fish into bite-size pieces. Add salmon and capers to potato mixture; toss gently.

Pour chicken broth mixture over salmon mixture, and toss gently. Spoon 1 cup salmon mixture onto each individual lettuce-lined salad plate. Top each serving with 1 tablespoon sour cream. Yield: 5 (1-cup) servings.

PER SERVING: 202 CALORIES (35% FROM FAT)
FAT 7.8G (SATURATED FAT 1.3G)
PROTEIN 17.3G CARBOHYDRATE 14.9G
CHOLESTEROL 44MG SODIUM 365MG

TUNA PASTA SALAD

4 ounces tri-color fusilli (corkscrew pasta),
    uncooked
1 cup frozen English peas, thawed
½ cup diced celery
½ cup diced carrot
½ cup minced fresh parsley
¼ cup diced green pepper
¼ cup diced sweet red pepper
¼ cup minced onion
¼ cup sliced ripe olives
2 cloves garlic, minced
1 (6-ounce) can low-sodium tuna in water,
    drained
½ cup nonfat mayonnaise
½ cup nonfat sour cream
1 tablespoon lemon juice
2 teaspoons Dijon mustard
¼ teaspoon pepper

Cook pasta according to package directions, omitting salt and fat. Drain pasta; rinse under cold water, and drain again. Place pasta in a large bowl. Add peas and next 9 ingredients, tossing gently.

Combine mayonnaise and remaining 4 ingredients in a small bowl, stirring well. Spoon mayonnaise mixture over pasta mixture, and toss well. Cover and chill thoroughly. Toss gently before serving. Yield: 4 (1½-cup) servings.

PER SERVING: 266 CALORIES (19% FROM FAT)
FAT 5.5G (SATURATED FAT 2.6G)
PROTEIN 15.3G CARBOHYDRATE 38.8G
CHOLESTEROL 21MG SODIUM 609MG

SALAD NIÇOISE FOR TWO

3 tablespoons white wine vinegar
2 tablespoons water
1½ teaspoons Dijon mustard
½ teaspoon olive oil
⅛ teaspoon freshly ground pepper
¼ pound fresh green beans
2 small round red potatoes (about ¼ pound)
2 tablespoons julienne-sliced sweet red pepper
1 tablespoon chopped purple onion
1 (6-ounce) tuna steak (¾ inch thick)
½ teaspoon olive oil
Vegetable cooking spray
2 cups torn fresh spinach
4 cherry tomatoes, quartered
1 tablespoon sliced ripe olives

Combine first 5 ingredients in a small jar; cover tightly, and shake vigorously. Set aside.

Wash beans; trim ends, and remove strings. Arrange in a steamer basket over boiling water. Cover; steam 5 minutes or until crisp-tender. Drain.

Wash potatoes. Cook in boiling water to cover 20 minutes or just until tender. Drain and cool slightly. Cut potatoes into ¼-inch-thick slices.

Combine potato, green beans, sweet red pepper, and onion; toss gently. Add half of vinegar mixture; toss gently. Cover and chill 2 hours.

Brush tuna steak with ½ teaspoon olive oil. Place on rack of a broiler pan coated with cooking spray. Broil 5½ inches from heat (with electric oven door partially opened) 3 to 4 minutes on each side or until fish flakes easily when tested with a fork. Flake fish into pieces.

Place spinach on a serving plate. Arrange green bean mixture, tuna, tomatoes, and olives evenly over spinach. Drizzle remaining vinegar mixture evenly over salad. Yield: 2 servings.

PER SERVING: 234 CALORIES (29% FROM FAT)
FAT 7.5G (SATURATED FAT 1.5G)
PROTEIN 23.4G CARBOHYDRATE 17.9G
CHOLESTEROL 33MG SODIUM 211MG

Salad Niçoise for Two

HARBOR SALAD
(pictured on page 46)

2 tablespoons sugar
2 tablespoons finely chopped walnuts
Vegetable cooking spray
1 teaspoon paprika
½ teaspoon ground cumin
½ teaspoon chili powder
¼ teaspoon salt
¼ teaspoon ground red pepper
3 (4-ounce) tuna steaks
1 cup torn romaine lettuce
1 cup torn leaf lettuce
1 cup torn iceberg lettuce
¼ cup sliced green onions
8 cherry tomatoes, quartered
Creamy Dressing

Sprinkle sugar in an even layer in a saucepan; place over medium heat. Cook, stirring constantly, until sugar melts and syrup is light brown. Stir in walnuts; cook until syrup becomes caramel colored. Immediately pour mixture out onto a piece of aluminum foil coated with cooking spray. Let cool; crush into small pieces. Set aside.

Combine paprika and next 4 ingredients. Rub mixture on both sides of each steak. Place a cast-iron skillet over medium-high heat until hot. Add steaks, and cook 3 minutes on each side or until fish flakes easily when tested with a fork. Remove from heat, and flake fish into bite-size pieces.

Place greens in a bowl. Add fish, green onions, and tomatoes; toss gently. Sprinkle with sugared walnuts. Drizzle with Creamy Dressing, and serve immediately. Yield: 4 servings.

CREAMY DRESSING
½ cup nonfat sour cream
¼ cup plain nonfat yogurt
1 tablespoon lemon juice

Combine all ingredients in a small bowl, stirring well. Yield: ¾ cup.

PER SERVING: 227 CALORIES (31% FROM FAT)
FAT 7.7G (SATURATED FAT 1.3G)
PROTEIN 25.0G CARBOHYDRATE 14.0G
CHOLESTEROL 33MG SODIUM 222MG

SPICY CRABMEAT SALAD IN TOMATO CUPS

¾ pound fresh lump crabmeat, drained
⅓ cup thinly sliced celery
2 tablespoons thinly sliced green onions
2 tablespoons plain nonfat yogurt
2 tablespoons nonfat mayonnaise
2 tablespoons no-salt-added tomato sauce
1 tablespoon white wine vinegar
¼ teaspoon cracked black pepper
¼ teaspoon hot sauce
⅛ teaspoon salt
⅛ teaspoon ground white pepper
1 large clove garlic, minced
4 medium tomatoes
4 Bibb lettuce leaves

Combine crabmeat, celery, and green onions in a medium bowl; toss gently, and set aside. Combine yogurt and next 8 ingredients; stir well. Add yogurt mixture to crabmeat mixture; stir well. Cover and chill 2 hours.

Core tomatoes; cut each tomato into 4 wedges, cutting to, but not through, base of tomato. Spread edges slightly apart. Spoon ½ cup crabmeat mixture into each tomato cup. Serve on individual lettuce-lined salad plates. Yield: 4 servings.

PER SERVING: 156 CALORIES (14% FROM FAT)
FAT 2.4G (SATURATED FAT 0.3G)
PROTEIN 19.5G CARBOHYDRATE 15.7G
CHOLESTEROL 82MG SODIUM 439MG

FYI

Do you love the taste of fresh crabmeat but dislike the price? Try imitation crabmeat made from surimi. Surimi is produced from inexpensive fish but is similar in taste and appearance to the more expensive crabmeat.

Imitation crabmeat is low in fat and cholesterol but higher in sodium than fresh crabmeat.

STONE CRAB CLAWS WITH CREAMY DIJON DRESSING

2 tablespoons nonfat mayonnaise
2 tablespoons nonfat sour cream
2 teaspoons dry white wine
2 teaspoons lemon juice
2 teaspoons Dijon mustard
1 teaspoon prepared horseradish
½ teaspoon prepared mustard
4 cups tightly packed watercress leaves
1 cup shredded iceberg lettuce
½ cup sliced radishes
2 tablespoons chopped pecans, toasted
3½ tablespoons commercial reduced-calorie
     Italian dressing
2 pounds cooked stone crab claws, chilled

Combine first 7 ingredients in a small bowl; cover and chill at least 3 hours.

Combine watercress and next 4 ingredients in a medium bowl. Toss well, and set aside.

Crack all sections of crab claw shells with a hammer or nutcracker except the black-tipped claw portion. Remove the cracked shell, leaving meat attached to the intact claw.

To serve, place 1¼ cups watercress mixture on each individual serving plate. Top evenly with crab claws, and serve with mustard mixture. Yield: 4 servings.

PER SERVING: 135 CALORIES (29% FROM FAT)
FAT 4.4G (SATURATED FAT 0.4G)
PROTEIN 17.7G   CARBOHYDRATE 5.1G
CHOLESTEROL 80MG   SODIUM 606MG

Stone crab claws are very large and have black tips. These claws are marketed cooked because if frozen raw, the meat sticks to the shell.

Use a hammer or seafood cracker to crack all sections of shell except the black-tipped portion. Remove cracked shell, leaving black-tipped portion intact.

For this recipe, place claws on watercress mixture and serve with mustard dressing.

Chilled Lobster Salad with Basil-Lime Salsa

CHILLED LOBSTER SALAD WITH BASIL-LIME SALSA

2 cups seeded, chopped unpeeled tomato
   (about 1 pound), divided
2 tablespoons fresh lime juice
1 tablespoon balsamic vinegar
1 tablespoon olive oil
1 small clove garlic, peeled
⅓ cup peeled, seeded, and diced cucumber
⅓ cup finely chopped green onions
2 tablespoons finely chopped fresh basil
¼ teaspoon salt
⅛ teaspoon pepper
2 to 3 ears fresh corn, cooked
4 cups tightly packed sliced romaine lettuce
1 cup tightly packed trimmed watercress
¾ pound cooked lobster meat, cut into
   bite-size pieces

Position knife blade in food processor bowl; add ½ cup tomato, lime juice, vinegar, oil, and garlic. Process until smooth. Pour mixture into a medium bowl; stir in remaining 1½ cups tomato, cucumber, and next 4 ingredients. Set aside.

Cut whole kernels from ears of corn to measure 2 cups. Combine corn, lettuce, and watercress in a large bowl; toss well. Add tomato mixture, and toss gently to coat. Divide evenly among 4 serving plates; top each with lobster. Yield: 4 servings.

PER SERVING: 183 CALORIES (25% FROM FAT)
FAT 5.1G (SATURATED FAT 0.8G)
PROTEIN 19.3G CARBOHYDRATE 17.4G
CHOLESTEROL 81MG SODIUM 171MG

LOBSTER-BROCCOLI SALAD WITH LEMON MAYONNAISE

6 cups small fresh broccoli flowerets (about 1 pound)
⅔ cup julienne-sliced sweet red pepper
½ pound cooked lobster meat, cut into bite-size pieces (about 2 [1¼-pound] Maine lobsters)
½ cup plain nonfat yogurt
¼ cup reduced-fat mayonnaise
½ teaspoon sugar
½ teaspoon grated lemon rind
2 tablespoons fresh lemon juice
¼ teaspoon salt
¼ teaspoon minced fresh dill
¼ teaspoon coarsely ground pepper
8 Boston lettuce leaves
Fresh dill sprigs (optional)

Arrange broccoli in a steamer basket over boiling water. Cover and steam 4 minutes or until crisp-tender; drain. Rinse under cold running water; drain. Combine broccoli, sweet red pepper, and lobster in a large bowl; toss well.

Combine yogurt and next 7 ingredients in a bowl, and stir well. Add to broccoli mixture, and toss well. Place 1½ cups salad on each of 4 lettuce-lined plates. Garnish with fresh dill sprigs, if desired. Yield: 4 servings.

Note: Steamed lobster meat is available in some supermarkets. Or you can cook whole lobsters: Fill an 8-quart stockpot two-thirds full with water. Add 2 tablespoons salt, and bring water to a boil. Plunge lobsters, one at a time, headfirst into water; return to a boil. Cover, reduce heat, and simmer 8 minutes. Remove from water, and let cool. Crack shells, and remove lobster meat.

PER SERVING: 200 CALORIES (21% FROM FAT)
FAT 4.6G (SATURATED FAT 1.3G)
PROTEIN 21.6G CARBOHYDRATE 22.6G
CHOLESTEROL 41MG SODIUM 596MG

SHRIMP SALAD IN PINEAPPLE BOATS

¾ cup soft tofu, drained (about 6 ounces)
1 tablespoon sugar
1 tablespoon fresh lemon juice
1 teaspoon curry powder
¼ teaspoon salt
⅛ teaspoon ground ginger
⅛ teaspoon dried crushed red pepper
¼ cup mango chutney
1 (5-pound) pineapple
3 cups water
1 pound unpeeled large fresh shrimp
¾ cup (3-inch) julienne-sliced sweet red pepper
1 (8-ounce) can sliced water chestnuts, drained

Combine first 7 ingredients in container of an electric blender; cover and process until smooth. Pour into a bowl; stir in chutney. Set aside.

Cut pineapple lengthwise into quarters, keeping leaves intact. Cut core from each quarter; discard core. Cut pulp from rind, using a sharp or curved knife. Cut pulp into cubes; reserve 3 cups, and set aside. Reserve remaining pineapple cubes for another use.

Bring water to a boil in a saucepan; add shrimp, and cook 3 to 5 minutes or until shrimp turn pink. Drain well; rinse with cold water, and chill. Peel and devein shrimp.

Combine reserved 3 cups pineapple cubes, shrimp, sweet red pepper, and water chestnuts in a bowl. Add tofu mixture; stir well. Spoon 1½ cups mixture into each pineapple shell. Yield: 4 servings.

PER SERVING: 256 CALORIES (12% FROM FAT)
FAT 3.4G (SATURATED FAT 0.5G)
PROTEIN 22.6G CARBOHYDRATE 35.8G
CHOLESTEROL 140MG SODIUM 324MG

Shrimp and Rice Salad

SHRIMP AND RICE SALAD

3 cups water
1 pound unpeeled medium-size fresh shrimp
2 cups cooked long-grain rice (cooked without salt or fat)
½ cup chopped celery
½ cup chopped green pepper
¼ cup sliced pimiento-stuffed olives
¼ cup chopped onion
2 tablespoons diced pimiento
3 tablespoons commercial oil-free Italian dressing
2 tablespoons reduced-fat mayonnaise
2 tablespoons prepared mustard
1 tablespoon lemon juice
1 teaspoon salt-free lemon-pepper seasoning
⅛ teaspoon pepper
Lettuce leaves
Fresh parsley sprigs (optional)
Cooked shrimp (optional)
Pimiento-stuffed olives (optional)

Bring water to a boil; add shrimp, and cook 3 to 5 minutes or until shrimp turn pink. Drain well; rinse with cold water. Chill. Peel and devein shrimp.

Combine shrimp, rice, and next 5 ingredients in a medium bowl. Combine Italian dressing and next 5 ingredients, stirring until well blended. Pour over shrimp mixture, and toss gently to coat. Cover and chill 3 to 4 hours.

Line a serving plate with lettuce leaves. Spoon salad onto plate. If desired, garnish with parsley, shrimp, and olives. Yield: 5 (1-cup) servings.

PER SERVING: 209 CALORIES (16% FROM FAT)
FAT 3.8G (SATURATED FAT 0.6G)
PROTEIN 17.3G   CARBOHYDRATE 25.6G
CHOLESTEROL 111MG   SODIUM 401MG

SEAFOOD AND FUSILLI SALAD

1 cup peeled, diced papaya
1½ tablespoons lemon juice
1½ tablespoons white wine vinegar
1 tablespoon olive oil
1 tablespoon chopped fresh dill
1 tablespoon chopped fresh tarragon
2 ounces fusilli (corkscrew pasta), uncooked
1 pound unpeeled medium-size fresh shrimp
1 cup dry white wine
4 cloves garlic, minced
½ pound bay scallops
1 cup thinly sliced sweet red pepper
1 cup diced celery
1 cup tightly packed watercress leaves
4 cups shredded romaine lettuce

Combine papaya, lemon juice, vinegar, and oil in container of an electric blender; cover and process until smooth. Add dill and tarragon; process until herbs are minced. Cover and chill papaya mixture at least 1 hour.

Cook pasta according to package directions, omitting salt and fat. Set aside. Peel and devein shrimp; set aside.

Combine wine and garlic in a large saucepan; bring to a boil. Cook 1 minute. Add scallops; cook 1 minute or until scallops are opaque, stirring frequently. Remove from heat. Transfer scallops to a large bowl, using a slotted spoon; reserve wine mixture in saucepan.

Return saucepan to heat; bring wine mixture to a boil. Add shrimp; cook 2 to 3 minutes or until shrimp turn pink. Drain well.

Add shrimp, pasta, sweet red pepper, celery, and watercress to scallops; toss gently. Cover and chill thoroughly.

Just before serving, add papaya mixture to seafood mixture; toss gently. Place shredded romaine lettuce evenly on individual salad plates. Top evenly with seafood mixture. Yield: 5 servings.

PER SERVING: 186 CALORIES (19% FROM FAT)
FAT 4.0G (SATURATED FAT 0.6G)
PROTEIN 21.0G   CARBOHYDRATE 16.0G
CHOLESTEROL 114MG   SODIUM 218MG

Fish Sandwiches with Onion Relish

FISH SANDWICHES WITH ONION RELISH

4 (4-ounce) amberjack fillets
½ cup dry white wine
2 tablespoons low-sodium soy sauce
1 teaspoon peeled, grated gingerroot
1 clove garlic, minced
Vegetable cooking spray
2 teaspoons olive oil
1 large onion, thinly sliced and separated into rings
2 teaspoons honey
2 teaspoons low-sodium soy sauce
¼ cup nonfat mayonnaise
½ teaspoon peeled, grated gingerroot
4 (2-ounce) French bread rolls, split and toasted
4 green leaf lettuce leaves

Place fillets in a shallow dish. Combine wine and next 3 ingredients in a small bowl, stirring well; set aside ¼ cup mixture. Pour remaining mixture over fillets. Cover fillets, and marinate in refrigerator 30 minutes.

Coat a large nonstick skillet with cooking spray; add oil. Place over medium-high heat until hot. Add onion; sauté 5 minutes or until tender. Stir in honey and 2 teaspoons soy sauce; set aside, and keep warm.

Remove fillets from marinade, discarding marinade in dish. Place fillets on rack of a broiler pan coated with cooking spray. Broil 5½ inches from heat (with electric oven door partially opened) 3 minutes. Turn fillets, and broil 3 additional minutes or until fish flakes easily when tested with a fork, basting occasionally with ¼ cup reserved wine mixture.

Combine mayonnaise and ½ teaspoon gingerroot; spread evenly on bottom halves of rolls. Top with lettuce and fillets; spoon onion mixture evenly over fillets and top with remaining bun halves. Serve immediately. Yield: 4 servings.

PER SERVING: 336 CALORIES (13% FROM FAT)
FAT 4.7G (SATURATED FAT 1.0G)
PROTEIN 27.8G   CARBOHYDRATE 41.3G
CHOLESTEROL 44MG   SODIUM 686MG

OVEN-FRIED CATFISH SANDWICHES

4 (4-ounce) farm-raised catfish fillets
½ teaspoon coarsely ground black pepper
⅔ cup corn flake crumbs
1 teaspoon paprika
4 egg whites, lightly beaten
Vegetable cooking spray
¼ cup commercial fat-free Thousand Island dressing
¼ cup nonfat sour cream
¼ teaspoon ground red pepper
4 reduced-calorie whole wheat hamburger buns
4 green leaf lettuce leaves
4 tomato slices

Sprinkle fillets with black pepper.

Combine corn flake crumbs and paprika in a small bowl, stirring well. Dip fillets in egg whites; dredge in cereal mixture. Place fillets on a baking sheet coated with cooking spray. Bake at 400° for 25 to 30 minutes or until fish flakes easily when tested with a fork.

Combine salad dressing, sour cream, and red pepper in a small bowl, stirring well. Spread salad dressing mixture evenly over top half of each bun. Place a lettuce leaf and a tomato slice on bottom half of each bun; top each with a fillet. Place remaining bun halves, coated side down, over fillets. Yield: 4 servings.

PER SERVING: 321 CALORIES (17% FROM FAT)
FAT 6.2G (SATURATED FAT 1.7G)
PROTEIN 29.6G   CARBOHYDRATE 33.7G
CHOLESTEROL 66MG   SODIUM 600MG

GRILLED GROUPER SANDWICHES WITH PINEAPPLE SALSA

1 (8¼-ounce) can crushed pineapple in juice, undrained
2 tablespoons sliced green onions
1 tablespoon finely chopped sweet red pepper
1 tablespoon lime juice
½ teaspoon sugar
½ teaspoon peeled, minced gingerroot
½ teaspoon dry mustard
Dash of ground white pepper
2 (4-ounce) grouper fillets (¾ inch thick)
Vegetable cooking spray
2 green leaf lettuce leaves
2 (2½-ounce) kaiser rolls, split and toasted

Drain pineapple, reserving juice. Combine 2 tablespoons pineapple juice, drained pineapple, green onions, and next 6 ingredients. Set aside.

Place fillets in a grilling basket coated with cooking spray. Place grill rack on grill over medium-hot coals (350° to 400°). Place basket on rack; grill, covered, 5 minutes on each side or until fish flakes easily when tested with a fork, basting frequently with 2 tablespoons reserved pineapple juice.

Place a lettuce leaf on bottom half of each roll; place fillets on lettuce. Spoon 3 tablespoons pineapple mixture over each fillet; top with remaining roll halves. Using a slotted spoon, serve remaining pineapple mixture with sandwiches. Yield: 2 servings.

PER SERVING: 401 CALORIES (14% FROM FAT)
FAT 6.1G (SATURATED FAT 0.9G)
PROTEIN 30.2G   CARBOHYDRATE 56.0G
CHOLESTEROL 42MG   SODIUM 517MG

Grilled Grouper Sandwiches with Pineapple Salsa

TUNA SANDWICH BOATS

4 (1½-ounce) sourdough French rolls
1 (3¼-ounce) can tuna in water, drained
2 tablespoons (½ ounce) shredded reduced-fat
    Cheddar cheese
1 tablespoon chopped water chestnuts
1 tablespoon chopped celery
1 tablespoon chopped green pepper
1 tablespoon slivered almonds, toasted
1½ teaspoons grated onion
1½ teaspoons sliced pimiento-stuffed olives
Dash of low-sodium Worcestershire sauce
1½ tablespoons nonfat mayonnaise

Cut a ½-inch slice off top of each roll; set tops aside. Hollow out center of rolls, leaving ½-inch-thick shells. Reserve excess bread for another use.

Combine tuna and remaining 9 ingredients, tossing gently. Spoon tuna mixture evenly into shells; cover with tops. Transfer sandwiches to a baking sheet. Bake at 400° for 15 minutes or until thoroughly heated; serve warm. Yield: 2 servings.

PER SERVING: 361 CALORIES (19% FROM FAT)
FAT 7.8G (SATURATED FAT 1.9G)
PROTEIN 20.3G CARBOHYDRATE 50.0G
CHOLESTEROL 22MG SODIUM 826MG

MANGO-CRAB SALAD SANDWICHES

¼ cup reduced-fat mayonnaise
1 tablespoon minced celery
1 tablespoon fresh cilantro
2 teaspoons fresh lemon juice
1 teaspoon chopped jalapeño pepper
⅔ cup diced peeled mango
1 (6-ounce) can crabmeat, drained
2 curly leaf lettuce leaves
1 English muffin, split and toasted
1 tablespoon slivered almonds, toasted

Combine first 5 ingredients in a bowl; stir well. Add mango and crabmeat; toss gently to coat.

Arrange 1 lettuce leaf on each muffin half, and top each with ¾ cup crab mixture. Sprinkle with almonds. Yield: 2 servings.

PER SERVING: 286 CALORIES (29% FROM FAT)
FAT 9.2G (SATURATED FAT 2.3G)
PROTEIN 16.2G CARBOHYDRATE 35.0G
CHOLESTEROL 54MG SODIUM 695MG

CRAB SALAD ON ENGLISH MUFFIN

½ cup light process cream cheese
2 tablespoons nonfat mayonnaise
1 tablespoon lemon juice
1 teaspoon prepared horseradish
1 teaspoon Dijon mustard
2 tablespoons chopped celery
1 tablespoon chopped green onions
1 tablespoon toasted sesame seeds
8 ounces fresh lump crabmeat, drained
3 English muffins, split and toasted
1 tablespoon chopped fresh parsley
⅛ teaspoon paprika
6 lemon wedges (optional)

Combine first 5 ingredients in a small bowl; stir well. Add celery, green onions, and sesame seeds; stir well. Stir in crabmeat. Spoon crab mixture evenly over English muffin halves. Broil 5½ inches from heat (with electric oven door partially opened) 3 to 4 minutes or until lightly browned.

Top each sandwich with parsley and paprika. Garnish with lemon wedges, if desired. Yield: 6 servings.

PER SERVING: 180 CALORIES (26% FROM FAT)
FAT 5.1G (SATURATED FAT 2.1G)
PROTEIN 12.5G CARBOHYDRATE 20.4G
CHOLESTEROL 49MG SODIUM 471MG

Creole Oyster Po' Boy

CREOLE OYSTER PO' BOYS

⅓ cup cornmeal
⅓ cup fine, dry breadcrumbs
½ teaspoon garlic powder
¼ teaspoon salt
¼ teaspoon ground red pepper
¼ teaspoon black pepper
2 tablespoons low-fat buttermilk
1 egg white
2 (10-ounce) containers standard oysters, drained
Vegetable cooking spray
1 (1-pound) loaf French bread (about 16 inches long)
Creole Mayonnaise
2 cups thinly sliced iceberg lettuce
24 thin slices tomato

Combine first 6 ingredients in a bowl; stir well. Combine buttermilk and egg white in a bowl; stir well. Dip oysters in buttermilk mixture, and dredge in cornmeal mixture.

Coat a large nonstick skillet with cooking spray, and place over medium heat until hot. Add oysters, and cook 3 minutes on each side or until browned.

Cut bread in half horizontally; spread Creole Mayonnaise over cut sides of bread. Arrange lettuce and tomato over bottom half of loaf; top with oysters and top half of loaf. Cut into 8 pieces. Serve immediately. Yield: 8 sandwiches.

CREOLE MAYONNAISE

¼ cup reduced-fat mayonnaise
1 tablespoon minced green onions
1 tablespoon minced fresh parsley
2 teaspoons sweet pickle relish
2 teaspoons Creole or other coarse-grained mustard
1 teaspoon capers
½ teaspoon hot sauce

Combine all ingredients in a bowl; stir well, and set aside. Yield: ⅓ cup.

PER SERVING: 285 CALORIES (15% FROM FAT)
FAT 4.8G (SATURATED FAT 1.3G)
PROTEIN 11.5G   CARBOHYDRATE 46.3G
CHOLESTEROL 35MG   SODIUM 655MG

SHRIMP-VEGETABLE PITA POCKETS

3 cups water
¾ pound unpeeled medium-size fresh shrimp
1 cup fresh snow pea pods
3 cups shredded fresh spinach
1½ cups sliced fresh mushrooms
1 cup bean sprouts
2 tablespoons red wine vinegar
1 tablespoon olive oil
1 teaspoon minced fresh garlic
½ teaspoon dry mustard
¼ teaspoon salt
⅛ teaspoon ground white pepper
3 (6-inch) pita bread rounds, cut in half crosswise

Bring water to a boil; add shrimp, and cook 3 to 5 minutes or until shrimp turn pink. Chill; peel and devein shrimp. Cut shrimp into ¾-inch pieces; set aside.

Wash snow peas; trim ends, remove strings, and cut in half. Combine snow peas, shrimp, spinach, mushrooms, and bean sprouts in a large bowl, and toss well.

Combine vinegar and next 5 ingredients in a small bowl; stir well using a wire whisk. Pour over shrimp mixture, and toss well. Spoon 1 cup mixture into each pita half. Serve immediately. Yield: 6 servings.

PER SERVING: 168 CALORIES (19% FROM FAT)
FAT 3.6G (SATURATED FAT 0.4G)
PROTEIN 9.7G   CARBOHYDRATE 22.7G
CHOLESTEROL 55MG   SODIUM 372MG

SHRIMP CALZONES

You'll need about 1 pound of unpeeled fresh shrimp to yield 8 ounces of cooked, peeled shrimp.

1 (1-pound) loaf commercial frozen white bread dough
1⅓ cups (8 ounces) chopped cooked shrimp (cooked without salt or seasonings)
1 cup chopped romaine lettuce
½ cup (2 ounces) shredded Muenster cheese
⅓ cup chopped purple onion
1 tablespoon dry white wine
2 teaspoons olive oil
⅛ teaspoon dried thyme
⅛ teaspoon pepper
3 cloves garlic, minced
Vegetable cooking spray

Thaw bread dough.

Combine shrimp, lettuce, cheese, and onion in a bowl; toss well. Combine wine and next 4 ingredients; stir well. Add to shrimp mixture; toss well.

Divide dough into 8 equal portions. Working with 1 portion at a time (cover remaining portions to keep dough from drying out), roll each portion to ⅛-inch thickness. Place on a large baking sheet coated with cooking spray, and pat each portion into a 6-inch circle with floured fingertips. Spoon ⅓ cup shrimp mixture onto half of each circle; moisten edges of dough with water. Fold dough over filling; press edges together with a fork to seal. Lightly coat with cooking spray.

Bake at 375° for 20 minutes or until golden. Remove from oven, and lightly coat again with cooking spray. Serve warm. Yield: 8 servings.

PER SERVING: 224 CALORIES (23% FROM FAT)
FAT 5.8G (SATURATED FAT 1.6G)
PROTEIN 12.9G   CARBOHYDRATE 29.7G
CHOLESTEROL 63MG   SODIUM 389MG

SHRIMP SALAD SANDWICHES

3 cups water
1 pound unpeeled medium-size fresh shrimp
¼ cup nonfat cream cheese, softened
2 tablespoons sliced green onions
2 tablespoons diced sweet red pepper
2 teaspoons nonfat mayonnaise
2 teaspoons lime juice
1 teaspoon capers
½ teaspoon dried dillweed
2 (2½-ounce) French rolls

Bring water to a boil; add shrimp, and cook 3 to 5 minutes or until shrimp turn pink. Drain well; rinse with cold water. Chill. Peel and devein shrimp.

Combine cream cheese and next 6 ingredients, stirring well. Add shrimp, and toss gently. Cover and chill 1 hour.

Cut a ½-inch slice off top of each roll; set tops aside. Hollow out center of rolls, leaving ½-inch-thick shells. Reserve excess bread for another use. Place bread shells and tops, cut sides up, on rack of a broiler pan. Broil 5½ inches from heat (with electric oven door partially opened) 1 to 2 minutes or until lightly toasted. Spoon shrimp mixture evenly into shells; cover with tops. Yield: 2 servings.

PER SERVING: 311 CALORIES (7% FROM FAT)
FAT 2.4G (SATURATED FAT 0.7G)
PROTEIN 33.2G   CARBOHYDRATE 35.0G
CHOLESTEROL 228MG   SODIUM 960MG

Grouper with Roasted Ratatouille (recipe on page 72)

FISH ENTRÉES

The traditional deep-frying method of preparing fish in shortening or oil has been replaced by several healthy cooking alternatives, including baking, broiling, and poaching. From amberjack to tuna, you'll find these recipes easier and tastier than ever—and suited to almost any occasion.

If it's supper for the family, turn to page 72 for Golden Fish Nuggets or page 73 for Oven-Poached Halibut. But when something fancier suits your dinner plans, try Braided Flounder with Tropical Relish (page 68) or Florentine Orange Roughy en Papillote (page 77).

Since overcooking is one of the most common problems in preparing fish, be sure to follow the recommended cooking times. Also be aware that an inaccurate oven temperature will cause the fish to cook either too quickly or too slowly. If you suspect a problem, buy an oven thermometer to check it out. (Refer to page 75 for more information on cooking fish.)

AMBERJACK WITH TOMATO-FENNEL SAUCE

Vegetable cooking spray
1 cup canned no-salt-added chicken broth, undiluted
½ cup chopped onion
½ cup chopped fennel bulb
1 teaspoon minced garlic
¼ teaspoon crushed fennel seeds
1 (14½-ounce) can no-salt-added stewed tomatoes, undrained
1 (8-ounce) can no-salt-added tomato sauce
¼ cup chopped fresh parsley, divided
½ teaspoon sugar
½ teaspoon freshly ground pepper, divided
¼ teaspoon salt
6 (4-ounce) amberjack fillets
4 cups water

Coat a large nonstick skillet with cooking spray; add chicken broth. Place over medium-high heat until hot. Add onion and next 3 ingredients; cook until vegetables are tender and liquid evaporates. Stir in stewed tomatoes and tomato sauce. Cook, uncovered, over low heat 30 minutes or until thickened, stirring occasionally. Stir in 2 tablespoons parsley, sugar, ¼ teaspoon pepper, and salt.

Sprinkle fillets with remaining ¼ teaspoon pepper. Bring water to a boil in a large nonstick skillet over medium heat. Reduce heat, and add fillets; cover and simmer 8 minutes or until fish flakes easily when tested with a fork. Remove fish from liquid, and place on a serving platter; discard liquid. Spoon tomato mixture evenly over fillets, and sprinkle with remaining 2 tablespoons parsley. Yield: 6 servings.

PER SERVING: 169 CALORIES (13% FROM FAT)
FAT 2.5G (SATURATED FAT 0.5G)
PROTEIN 25.8G   CARBOHYDRATE 10.2G
CHOLESTEROL 49MG   SODIUM 163MG

SOUTH-OF-THE-BORDER BASS

For a quick and easy low-fat meal, serve commercial yellow rice and steamed broccoli with these spicy fillets.

Olive oil-flavored vegetable cooking spray
1 teaspoon olive oil
1 cup finely chopped onion
1 tablespoon chili powder
2 teaspoons minced garlic
¼ teaspoon ground cumin
¼ teaspoon ground coriander
1 (14½-ounce) can no-salt-added whole tomatoes, undrained and chopped
¼ cup finely chopped ripe olives
¼ cup fresh lemon juice
1 tablespoon honey
½ teaspoon coarsely ground pepper
6 (4-ounce) sea bass fillets
½ cup chopped fresh parsley

Coat a large nonstick skillet with cooking spray; add oil. Place over medium-high heat until hot. Add onion and next 4 ingredients; sauté 3 minutes or until onion is tender. Add tomatoes and next 4 ingredients. Bring to a boil; cover, reduce heat, and simmer 15 minutes, stirring occasionally.

Place fillets in an 11- x 7- x 1½-inch baking dish coated with cooking spray; spoon tomato mixture over fillets. Cover and bake at 350° for 20 to 25 minutes or until fish flakes easily when tested with a fork. Sprinkle with parsley. Yield: 6 servings.

PER SERVING: 190 CALORIES (29% FROM FAT)
FAT 6.2G (SATURATED FAT 1.2G)
PROTEIN 22.7G   CARBOHYDRATE 11.1G
CHOLESTEROL 77MG   SODIUM 166MG

Cajun Catfish

CAJUN CATFISH

4 (4-ounce) farm-raised catfish fillets
1 tablespoon fresh lemon juice
1 tablespoon plus 1 teaspoon Cajun Seasoning
Vegetable cooking spray
Lemon wedges (optional)

Brush both sides of fillets with lemon juice, and sprinkle with Cajun Seasoning. Place fish on rack of a broiler pan coated with cooking spray, and broil 5½ inches from heat (with electric oven door partially opened) 5 minutes on each side or until fish flakes easily when tested with a fork. Serve with lemon wedges, if desired. Yield: 4 servings.

CAJUN SEASONING

2½ tablespoons paprika
1 tablespoon plus 1 teaspoon dried oregano
1 teaspoon salt
1 teaspoon garlic powder
1 teaspoon ground white pepper
1 teaspoon black pepper
1 teaspoon ground red pepper

Combine all ingredients in a zip-top plastic bag. Seal bag; shake well. Store tightly sealed. Yield: ⅓ cup.

PER SERVING: 140 CALORIES (33% FROM FAT)
FAT 5.1G (SATURATED FAT 1.2G)
PROTEIN 20.1G   CARBOHYDRATE 1.5G
CHOLESTEROL 66MG   SODIUM 219MG

CODFISH CAKES WITH TARTAR SAUCE

6 cups water
1 pound cod fillets
¾ cup soft breadcrumbs
3 tablespoons minced fresh parsley
3 tablespoons minced green pepper
3 tablespoons thinly sliced green onions
2 tablespoons nonfat mayonnaise
1 tablespoon lemon juice
1½ teaspoons low-sodium Worcestershire
    sauce
⅛ teaspoon coarsely ground pepper
1 egg, lightly beaten
Vegetable cooking spray
2 teaspoons margarine, divided
Tartar Sauce

Bring water to a boil in a large skillet over medium heat. Reduce heat, and add fillets; cover and simmer 6 minutes or until fish flakes easily when tested with a fork. Drain well; pat dry.

Flake fish with a fork, and place in a bowl. Add breadcrumbs and next 8 ingredients; stir gently. Divide mixture into 6 equal portions, shaping each into a ½-inch-thick patty.

Coat skillet with cooking spray. Add 1 teaspoon margarine; place over medium heat until melted. Add 3 patties; cook 3 minutes on each side. Remove fish from skillet. Set aside; keep warm. Repeat procedure with remaining 1 teaspoon margarine and 3 patties. Serve with Tartar Sauce. Yield: 6 servings.

TARTAR SAUCE

3 tablespoons plain low-fat yogurt
2 tablespoons nonfat mayonnaise
1½ tablespoons sweet pickle relish
1 teaspoon lemon juice
⅛ teaspoon dried tarragon

Combine all ingredients in a bowl; stir well. Cover and chill. Yield: ¼ cup plus 2 tablespoons.

PER SERVING: 125 CALORIES (22% FROM FAT)
FAT 3.1G (SATURATED FAT 0.7G)
PROTEIN 15.6G   CARBOHYDRATE 8.0G
CHOLESTEROL 70MG   SODIUM 264MG

BRAIDED FLOUNDER WITH TROPICAL RELISH

6 (4-ounce) flounder fillets
Vegetable cooking spray
3 tablespoons lemon juice
¾ pound fresh spinach
Tropical Relish
Lemon rind strips (optional)
Lime rind strips (optional)

Place fillets on a baking sheet coated with cooking spray. Cut each fillet lengthwise into 3 equal strips, leaving about 1 inch at one end of each fillet connected. Braid strips; tuck ends under. Brush fillets with lemon juice. Broil 5½ inches from heat (with electric oven door partially opened) 6 to 8 minutes or until fish flakes easily when tested with a fork.

Remove stems from spinach; wash leaves thoroughly. Arrange spinach in a steamer basket over boiling water. Cover and steam 1 to 2 minutes or just until spinach wilts.

Arrange spinach on individual plates. Place a fillet in center of each plate. Spoon Tropical Relish around fillets. If desired, garnish with lemon and lime rind strips. Yield: 6 servings.

TROPICAL RELISH

1 cup diced fresh pineapple
1 cup diced cantaloupe
½ cup diced ripe mango
¼ cup chopped purple onion
1 (7-ounce) jar roasted red peppers in water,
    drained and chopped
2 tablespoons white wine vinegar
1 tablespoon minced fresh cilantro
1 tablespoon lime juice

Combine all ingredients in a medium bowl, and toss gently. Cover relish, and chill at least 1 hour. Yield: 3 cups.

PER SERVING: 176 CALORIES (11% FROM FAT)
FAT 2.2G (SATURATED FAT 0.4G)
PROTEIN 24.0G   CARBOHYDRATE 16.6G
CHOLESTEROL 60MG   SODIUM 146MG

Braided Flounder with Tropical Relish

CRABMEAT-STUFFED FLOUNDER

Vegetable cooking spray
1 teaspoon reduced-calorie margarine
¼ cup chopped green onions
¼ pound fresh lump crabmeat, drained
½ cup soft French breadcrumbs
¼ cup chopped fresh parsley
¼ cup plain nonfat yogurt
1 teaspoon dried oregano
1 teaspoon lemon juice
4 (3-ounce) flounder fillets
2 teaspoons reduced-calorie margarine, melted
¼ cup grated Romano cheese

Coat a small nonstick skillet with cooking spray; add 1 teaspoon margarine. Place over medium-high heat until margarine melts. Add green onions, and sauté 1 minute. Add crabmeat and next 5 ingredients; stir well.

Spoon ¼ cup crabmeat mixture in center of each fillet; roll up each fillet, jellyroll fashion, beginning at narrow end. Secure with wooden picks. Place rolls, seam side down, in an 8-inch square baking dish coated with cooking spray. Brush evenly with 2 teaspoons melted margarine.

Bake flounder rolls, uncovered, at 350° for 10 minutes. Sprinkle cheese evenly over flounder rolls; bake 10 additional minutes or until fish flakes easily when tested with a fork. To serve, transfer to a serving platter, and remove wooden picks. Yield: 4 servings.

PER SERVING: 184 CALORIES (28% FROM FAT)
FAT 5.7G (SATURATED FAT 1.8G)
PROTEIN 25.7G   CARBOHYDRATE 6.4G
CHOLESTEROL 77MG   SODIUM 316MG

FLOUNDER WITH CAPERED WINE SAUCE

½ cup plus 1 tablespoon dry white wine
1 teaspoon lemon zest
⅓ cup fresh lemon juice
1 teaspoon dried Italian seasoning
4 (4-ounce) flounder fillets
Olive oil-flavored cooking spray
2 cloves garlic, minced
1 teaspoon all-purpose flour
⅓ cup dry white wine
2 tablespoons fresh lemon juice
1½ tablespoons chopped fresh parsley
1½ teaspoons capers
1 tablespoon freshly grated Parmesan cheese

Combine first 4 ingredients in a large heavy-duty, zip-top plastic bag. Add fillets; seal bag, and shake until fish is well coated. Marinate in refrigerator 30 minutes.

Coat a small saucepan with cooking spray; place over medium heat until hot. Add garlic, and sauté 10 seconds. Add flour; cook, stirring constantly with a wire whisk, 1 minute. Gradually add ⅓ cup wine and 2 tablespoons lemon juice, stirring constantly. Cook, stirring constantly, 1 to 2 minutes or until thickened and bubbly. Stir in parsley and capers. Set aside, and keep warm.

Remove fish from marinade; discard marinade. Place fish on rack of a broiler pan coated with cooking spray. Broil 5½ inches from heat (with electric oven door partially opened) 2 minutes. Sprinkle fish with cheese, and broil 2 minutes or until fish flakes easily when tested with a fork. Serve fish with wine sauce. Yield: 4 servings.

PER SERVING: 173 CALORIES (16% FROM FAT)
FAT 3.0G (SATURATED FAT 0.9G)
PROTEIN 23.2G   CARBOHYDRATE 4.4G
CHOLESTEROL 63MG   SODIUM 238MG

GROUPER WITH FRUIT AND PEPPER SALSA

½ cup chopped fresh pineapple
⅓ cup chopped green pepper
⅓ cup chopped sweet red pepper
⅓ cup chopped sweet yellow pepper
1 kiwifruit, peeled and thinly sliced
1 tablespoon white wine vinegar
1 teaspoon brown sugar
1 teaspoon peeled, grated gingerroot
1½ teaspoons water
⅛ teaspoon dried crushed red pepper
2 tablespoons lemon juice
¼ teaspoon curry powder
⅛ teaspoon salt
3 (8-ounce) grouper fillets, halved
Vegetable cooking spray

Combine first 10 ingredients; cover and chill at least 2 hours.

Combine lemon juice, curry powder, and salt. Place fillets on rack of a broiler pan coated with cooking spray; brush with lemon juice mixture. Broil 5½ inches from heat (with electric oven door partially opened) 4 minutes on each side or until fish flakes easily when tested with a fork. Transfer fillets to a serving platter; top evenly with pineapple mixture. Yield: 6 servings.

PER SERVING: 140 CALORIES (10% FROM FAT)
FAT 1.6G (SATURATED FAT 0.3G)
PROTEIN 24.6G   CARBOHYDRATE 5.8G
CHOLESTEROL 46MG   SODIUM 102MG

Grouper with Fruit and Pepper Salsa

GROUPER WITH ROASTED RATATOUILLE

(pictured on page 64)

1 (1-pound) eggplant
1 medium-size sweet red pepper
1 medium-size sweet yellow pepper
1 medium zucchini
2 small yellow squash
1 cup chopped sweet onion
2 cloves garlic, minced
Olive oil-flavored vegetable cooking spray
2 teaspoons minced fresh rosemary
¼ teaspoon salt
2 (8-ounce) grouper fillets, cut into 1½-inch
    pieces
½ cup seeded, diced plum tomato
1 tablespoon balsamic vinegar
½ teaspoon freshly ground pepper
¼ pound fresh spinach leaves
Fresh rosemary sprigs (optional)

Peel eggplant; cut eggplant and peppers into 1-inch pieces. Cut zucchini and squash lengthwise into quarters; cut into 1-inch pieces. Combine eggplant, peppers, zucchini, squash, onion, and garlic in a 15- x 10- x 1-inch jellyroll pan; coat with cooking spray, and toss gently. Sprinkle minced rosemary and salt over vegetable mixture; toss gently.

Bake vegetables at 400° for 25 minutes or until tender, stirring occasionally. Add fillets; bake 12 additional minutes or until fish flakes easily when tested with a fork. Drain well.

Combine tomato, vinegar, and pepper. Add to fish mixture; toss gently. Arrange spinach leaves on individual serving plates; spoon fish mixture over spinach. Garnish with rosemary sprigs, if desired. Yield: 6 servings.

PER SERVING: 132 CALORIES (12% FROM FAT)
FAT 1.7G (SATURATED FAT 0.3G)
PROTEIN 17.6G CARBOHYDRATE 12.9G
CHOLESTEROL 28MG SODIUM 161MG

Golden Fish Nuggets with Dilled Tartar Sauce

GOLDEN FISH NUGGETS WITH DILLED TARTAR SAUCE

1 tablespoon reduced-calorie mayonnaise
1 tablespoon plain nonfat yogurt
2 teaspoons sweet pickle relish
½ teaspoon lemon juice
⅛ teaspoon onion powder
⅛ teaspoon dried dillweed
3 tablespoons corn flake crumbs
1 tablespoon grated Parmesan cheese
½ teaspoon paprika
⅛ teaspoon salt
1 egg white, lightly beaten
½ pound grouper or other firm white fish
    fillets, cut into 1-inch pieces
Vegetable cooking spray

Combine first 6 ingredients in a bowl; stir well. Cover and chill.

Combine corn flake crumbs and next 3 ingredients

in a shallow bowl; set crumb mixture aside.

Place egg white in a shallow bowl. Dip fish in egg white, and dredge in crumb mixture. Place on a baking sheet coated with cooking spray. Bake at 500° for 8 minutes or until crispy and browned. Serve with sauce. Serve with carrot and celery sticks, if desired. Yield: 2 servings.

PER SERVING: 164 CALORIES (24% FROM FAT)
FAT 4.4G (SATURATED FAT 0.9G)
PROTEIN 25.4G   CARBOHYDRATE 4.5G
CHOLESTEROL 47MG   SODIUM 392MG

FISH VERACRUZ

¼ cup unsweetened orange juice, divided
2 teaspoons chili powder
½ teaspoon garlic powder
¼ teaspoon salt
1 pound grouper or other white fish fillets
    (about 1 inch thick)
Vegetable cooking spray
2 cups cherry tomato halves
¼ cup thinly sliced green onions
2 tablespoons sliced ripe olives
2 tablespoons chopped fresh cilantro
2 tablespoons cider vinegar
2 teaspoons minced serrano chile pepper

Combine 2 tablespoons orange juice, chili powder, garlic powder, and salt in a bowl; stir well. Cut fillets into 4 equal portions; brush orange juice mixture over both sides of fish. Place on rack of a broiler pan coated with cooking spray.

Combine remaining 2 tablespoons orange juice, tomatoes, and remaining 5 ingredients in a bowl; toss well, and set aside. Broil fish 5½ inches from heat (with electric oven door partially opened) 4 minutes on each side or until fish flakes easily when tested with a fork. Serve with tomato mixture. Yield: 4 servings.

PER SERVING: 145 CALORIES (14% FROM FAT)
FAT 2.3G (SATURATED FAT 0.4G)
PROTEIN 23.3G   CARBOHYDRATE 8.2G
CHOLESTEROL 42MG   SODIUM 253MG

OVEN-POACHED HALIBUT

This recipe uses a moderate oven temperature to accomplish the same results as cooktop poaching.

Vegetable cooking spray
1 cup dry white wine
6 (6-ounce) halibut steaks
6 cups diced tomato
2 cups finely chopped onion
¼ cup chopped fresh basil or 1 tablespoon plus
    1 teaspoon dried basil
¼ cup chopped fresh parsley
2 tablespoons minced kalamata olives
1 tablespoon olive oil
½ teaspoon salt
½ teaspoon anchovy paste
⅛ teaspoon pepper
2 cloves garlic, minced
¼ cup dry breadcrumbs
1 tablespoon grated Parmesan cheese
1 teaspoon olive oil

Coat a 13- x 9- x 2-inch baking dish with cooking spray. Pour wine into dish, and arrange halibut steaks in dish. Combine tomato and next 9 ingredients in a bowl; stir well, and spoon over steaks. Bake at 350° for 35 minutes or until fish flakes easily when tested with a fork.

Combine breadcrumbs, cheese, and 1 teaspoon oil in a bowl; stir well. Sprinkle over tomato mixture, and broil fish 5½ inches from heat (with electric oven door partially opened) until crumbs are golden. Yield: 6 servings.

PER SERVING: 305 CALORIES (25% FROM FAT)
FAT 8.6G (SATURATED FAT 1.3G)
PROTEIN 38.9G   CARBOHYDRATE 17.9G
CHOLESTEROL 81MG   SODIUM 446MG

Mahimahi with Papaya and Roasted Red Pepper

MAHIMAHI WITH PAPAYA AND ROASTED RED PEPPER

1 teaspoon cornstarch
1 tablespoon water
2 teaspoons reduced-calorie margarine
1 tablespoon finely chopped shallots
1 (7-ounce) jar roasted red peppers in water,
    drained and cut into very thin strips
1 cup peeled, chopped ripe papaya
1 teaspoon minced jalapeño pepper
3 tablespoons fresh lime juice, divided
1 teaspoon reduced-calorie margarine, melted
4 (4-ounce) mahimahi fillets
Butter-flavored vegetable cooking spray
3 tablespoons chopped pistachios, divided

Combine cornstarch and water; set aside.
Melt 2 teaspoons margarine in a large skillet over medium heat. Add shallots, and sauté 2 minutes. Add red pepper, papaya, and jalapeño pepper; sauté 2 minutes. Add cornstarch mixture and 2 tablespoons lime juice; cook, stirring constantly, until thickened. Remove from heat, and keep warm.

Combine remaining 1 tablespoon lime juice and 1 teaspoon melted margarine; stir well. Place fillets on rack of a broiler pan coated with cooking spray, and brush with lime juice mixture. Broil 5½ inches from heat (with electric oven door partially opened) 4 minutes on each side. Sprinkle fillets with 2 tablespoons plus 1 teaspoon pistachios, pressing nuts into flesh of fish. Broil 3 additional minutes or until fish flakes easily when tested with a fork.

Serve with red pepper sauce; sprinkle with remaining 2 teaspoons pistachios. Yield: 4 servings.

PER SERVING: 172 CALORIES (30% FROM FAT)
FAT 5.7G (SATURATED FAT 0.7G)
PROTEIN 22.0G   CARBOHYDRATE 8.9G
CHOLESTEROL 49MG   SODIUM 102MG

BAKED MAHIMAHI WITH TOMATILLO SALSA

½ cup husked, finely chopped tomatillos
½ cup seeded, finely chopped yellow tomato
¼ cup minced green onions
3 tablespoons minced fresh cilantro
1 tablespoon seeded, minced jalapeño pepper
½ teaspoon ground cumin
¼ teaspoon salt
¼ teaspoon pepper
1½ tablespoons lemon juice
1 teaspoon dark sesame oil
4 (4-ounce) mahimahi fillets
Olive oil-flavored vegetable cooking spray

Combine first 8 ingredients in a small bowl; stir well. Cover and chill thoroughly.

Combine lemon juice and sesame oil; brush mixture evenly over both sides of each fillet. Place fillets in an 11- x 7- x 1½-inch baking dish coated with cooking spray. Bake, uncovered, at 450° for 10 minutes or until fish flakes easily when tested with a fork. Transfer to a serving platter. Spoon tomatillo mixture evenly over fillets. Yield: 4 servings.

PER SERVING: 124 CALORIES (17% FROM FAT)
FAT 2.4G (SATURATED FAT 0.4G)
PROTEIN 21.7G CARBOHYDRATE 3.5G
CHOLESTEROL 84MG SODIUM 254MG

Time It Right

When cooking fish, remember the "10-minute rule." Allow 10 minutes of cooking time for each 1 inch of thickness. (Measure at the thickest point.) To prevent the thin end of a fillet from overcooking, fold it under to create a more uniform thickness.

If the fish is frozen, double the cooking time; add 5 minutes if it is wrapped in foil or covered in a sauce. (This rule applies to baking at 450°, broiling, grilling, steaming, and poaching, but not to microwaving.)

ORANGE ROUGHY IN CHUNKY TOMATO SAUCE

2 tablespoons lemon juice
6 (4-ounce) orange roughy fillets
Olive oil-flavored vegetable cooking spray
2 teaspoons olive oil, divided
1 cup chopped purple onion
⅓ cup chopped sweet yellow pepper
⅓ cup chopped green pepper
1 tablespoon chopped garlic
2¼ cups sliced fresh mushrooms
2 cups peeled, seeded, and chopped tomato
½ cup dry white wine
½ cup water
2 tablespoons no-salt-added tomato paste
1 teaspoon dried basil
½ teaspoon dried oregano
¼ teaspoon salt
¼ teaspoon ground red pepper
2 tablespoons chopped fresh parsley

Pour lemon juice into a large shallow dish. Place fillets in a single layer in dish, turning to coat. Cover and marinate in refrigerator 30 minutes, turning fillets once.

Remove fish from marinade, discarding marinade. Coat a large nonstick skillet with cooking spray; add 1 teaspoon oil. Place over medium-high heat until hot. Add fillets; cook 2 minutes on each side or until lightly browned. Remove fish from skillet, and set aside.

Wipe skillet dry with a paper towel. Coat skillet with cooking spray; add remaining 1 teaspoon oil. Place over medium-high heat until hot. Add onion and chopped peppers; sauté 3 minutes. Add garlic, and sauté 1 minute.

Add mushrooms and next 8 ingredients; stir well. Bring to a boil; cover, reduce heat, and simmer 5 minutes. Stir in parsley. Add fillets; cover and simmer 10 minutes or until fish flakes easily when tested with a fork. Yield: 6 servings.

PER SERVING: 133 CALORIES (20% FROM FAT)
FAT 2.9G (SATURATED FAT 0.3G)
PROTEIN 18.6G CARBOHYDRATE 8.4G
CHOLESTEROL 23MG SODIUM 180MG

Florentine Orange Roughy en Papillote

Layer the ingredients near the crease of the parchment-paper heart. This leaves enough room for sealing the edges.

Pleat and crimp the edges of the parchment heart firmly to form a tight seal.

To serve, use scissors to cut a large opening in the top of the parchment packet, and fold back the corners.

FLORENTINE ORANGE ROUGHY EN PAPILLOTE

18 cherry tomatoes, halved
½ cup chopped green onions
¼ cup lemon juice
1 (10-ounce) package frozen chopped spinach, thawed
Vegetable cooking spray
¾ pound fresh mushrooms, sliced
2 cloves garlic, minced
¼ teaspoon salt
6 (4-ounce) orange roughy fillets
12 lemon slices

Combine first 3 ingredients. Cover and chill at least 1 hour.

Drain spinach, and press between paper towels. Set aside.

Cut 6 (15- x 12-inch) rectangles of parchment paper; fold in half lengthwise. Trim each into a heart shape. Place on baking sheets; open out flat.

Coat a large nonstick skillet with cooking spray; place over medium-high heat until hot. Add mushrooms and garlic; sauté 3 to 4 minutes or until tender. Stir in spinach and salt. Place one-sixth of spinach mixture on one half of each parchment heart near the crease; place fillets on spinach mixture. Spoon tomato mixture evenly over fillets; top each with 2 lemon slices.

Fold paper edges over to seal. Starting with rounded edges of hearts, pleat and crimp edges of parchment to make an airtight seal. Bake at 450° for 10 minutes or until bags are puffed and lightly browned.

Place packets on individual serving plates. Cut an opening in the top of each packet, and fold paper back. Serve immediately. Yield: 6 servings.

PER SERVING: 120 CALORIES (11% FROM FAT)
FAT 1.4G (SATURATED FAT 0.1G)
PROTEIN 19.8G   CARBOHYDRATE 8.3G
CHOLESTEROL 23MG   SODIUM 212MG

ORANGE ROUGHY IN POTATO CRUST

Frozen hash brown potato makes a crispy, low-fat coating for these seasoned fish fillets.

2⅔ cups frozen hash brown potato, thawed
¼ cup finely chopped onion
¼ cup frozen egg substitute, thawed
¼ teaspoon salt
¼ teaspoon pepper
Butter-flavored vegetable cooking spray
4 (4-ounce) orange roughy fillets
¼ teaspoon dried thyme
¼ teaspoon paprika
⅛ teaspoon salt
⅛ teaspoon garlic powder
⅛ teaspoon ground red pepper
1 tablespoon plus 1 teaspoon margarine, divided

Combine first 5 ingredients in a medium bowl. Coat 4 (12-inch) squares of aluminum foil with cooking spray. Place ⅓ cup potato mixture in center of each foil square, spreading to about ¼-inch thickness; top potato mixture with fillets. Set aside remaining potato mixture.

Combine thyme and next 4 ingredients. Sprinkle evenly over fillets.

Spoon remaining potato mixture evenly over fillets. Press mixture around fillets to seal. Fold foil over potato mixture, and freeze 1 hour or until potato mixture is firm.

Coat a large nonstick skillet with cooking spray; add 2 teaspoons margarine. Place over medium-high heat until margarine melts. Unwrap fillets, and place in skillet. Cook 7 minutes or until browned. Add remaining 2 teaspoons margarine. Turn fillets, and cook 5 additional minutes or until browned and fish flakes easily when tested with a fork. Yield: 4 servings.

PER SERVING: 181 CALORIES (24% FROM FAT)
FAT 4.9G (SATURATED FAT 0.8G)
PROTEIN 19.3G   CARBOHYDRATE 14.0G
CHOLESTEROL 23MG   SODIUM 365MG

HERBED SALMON FILLETS

2 tablespoons lemon juice
1 tablespoon low-sodium Worcestershire sauce
6 (4-ounce) salmon fillets
2 tablespoons soft French breadcrumbs
2 tablespoons grated Romano cheese
2 teaspoons minced garlic
1 teaspoon dried oregano
½ teaspoon dried tarragon
½ teaspoon dried marjoram
Butter-flavored vegetable cooking spray
2 teaspoons reduced-calorie margarine
Fresh oregano sprigs (optional)

Combine lemon juice and Worcestershire sauce in a small bowl. Place fillets in an 11- x 7- x 1½-inch baking dish; pour lemon juice mixture over fillets. Cover and marinate in refrigerator 1 hour.

Combine breadcrumbs and next 5 ingredients in a small bowl; set aside.

Remove fillets from marinade; discard marinade. Coat a large nonstick skillet with cooking spray; add margarine. Place over medium-high heat until margarine melts. Add fillets, and cook 1 to 2 minutes on each side or until lightly browned.

Coat baking dish with cooking spray, and add fillets. Sprinkle breadcrumb mixture evenly over fillets. Bake, uncovered, at 400° for 15 minutes or until fish flakes easily when tested with a fork. Garnish with fresh oregano sprigs, if desired. Yield: 6 servings.

PER SERVING: 156 CALORIES (32% FROM FAT)
FAT 5.5G (SATURATED FAT 1.1G)
PROTEIN 23.6G CARBOHYDRATE 2.0G
CHOLESTEROL 61MG SODIUM 146MG

CREOLE RED SNAPPER

1 tablespoon olive oil
¼ cup chopped onion
¼ cup chopped green pepper
1 clove garlic, minced
1 (14½-ounce) can no-salt-added whole tomatoes, undrained and chopped
2 teaspoons low-sodium Worcestershire sauce
2 teaspoons red wine vinegar
½ teaspoon dried basil
¼ teaspoon salt
¼ teaspoon freshly ground pepper
Dash of hot sauce
4 (4-ounce) red snapper fillets
Fresh basil sprigs (optional)

Heat oil in a large nonstick skillet over medium-high heat until hot. Add onion, green pepper, and garlic; sauté until tender.

Add tomatoes and next 6 ingredients. Bring to a boil; add fillets, spooning tomato mixture over fish. Reduce heat; cover and simmer 12 minutes or until fish flakes easily when tested with a fork. Garnish with basil sprigs, if desired. Yield: 4 servings.

PER SERVING: 173 CALORIES (26% FROM FAT)
FAT 5.0G (SATURATED FAT 0.8G)
PROTEIN 24.3G CARBOHYDRATE 6.9G
CHOLESTEROL 42MG SODIUM 243MG

Did You Know?

Some types of fish contain high amounts of omega-3 fatty acids, which are a type of polyunsaturated fat found in fish that have dark, moist flesh. These fatty acids may help reduce the chance of a heart attack by making blood platelets less likely to clump together and attach to blood vessel walls.

Fish with the highest amounts of omega-3 fatty acids include anchovies, herring, mackerel, pompano, sablefish, salmon, sardines, lake trout, tuna, and whitefish.

Creole Red Snapper

RED SNAPPER PARMIGIANA

½ cup dry white wine
½ teaspoon dried thyme
¼ teaspoon dried crushed red pepper
3 cloves garlic, crushed
4 (4-ounce) red snapper fillets (1 inch thick)
¼ cup all-purpose flour
¼ cup freshly grated Parmesan or Romano
   cheese
¼ teaspoon salt
¼ teaspoon pepper
Vegetable cooking spray
1½ teaspoons olive oil
Lemon wedges

Combine first 4 ingredients in a large heavy-duty, zip-top plastic bag. Add fillets. Seal bag; marinate in refrigerator 30 minutes, turning bag occasionally. Remove fillets from bag; discard marinade. Set fillets aside.

Combine flour and next 3 ingredients in a large zip-top plastic bag. Add fillets; seal bag, and shake to coat fillets with flour mixture.

Coat a large nonstick skillet with cooking spray; add oil, and place over medium heat until hot. Add fillets, and cook 6 minutes on each side or until fish flakes easily when tested with a fork. Serve with lemon wedges. Yield: 4 servings.

PER SERVING: 188 CALORIES (25% FROM FAT)
FAT 5.3G (SATURATED FAT 1.7G)
PROTEIN 26.6G   CARBOHYDRATE 6.1G
CHOLESTEROL 47MG   SODIUM 333MG

Red Snapper Parmigiana

SNAPPER AU GRATIN

1 pound red snapper fillets
½ teaspoon freshly ground black pepper,
    divided
Vegetable cooking spray
½ cup dry white wine
½ cup water
1½ tablespoons lemon juice, divided
6 cups sliced fresh mushrooms
2 small zucchini, thinly sliced
1 large sweet red pepper, chopped
¼ teaspoon salt
½ cup minced celery
2 tablespoons minced green onions
¼ teaspoon dried crushed red pepper
1 cup evaporated skimmed milk, divided
¼ cup all-purpose flour
½ cup minced fresh parsley
½ cup (2 ounces) shredded Cheddar cheese

Sprinkle fillets with ¼ teaspoon black pepper. Place in a 13- x 9- x 2-inch baking dish coated with cooking spray. Combine wine and water; pour over fillets. Bake, uncovered, at 400° for 12 minutes. Drain, pouring liquid into a glass measure; let solids settle. Reserve ¾ cup clear liquid.

Coat a nonstick skillet with cooking spray; add ¼ cup reserved liquid and 1 tablespoon lemon juice. Place over medium-high heat until hot. Add mushrooms; sauté 3 minutes. Add zucchini and sweet red pepper; sauté 3 minutes. Stir in salt and remaining ¼ teaspoon black pepper. Spoon over fillets.

Combine ¼ cup reserved liquid, celery, and next 2 ingredients in a saucepan. Bring to a boil. Reduce heat; simmer until tender. Combine ¼ cup evaporated milk and flour; stir until smooth. Stir in remaining ¾ cup evaporated milk and remaining ¼ cup reserved liquid; stir into celery mixture. Cook, stirring constantly, 2 minutes. Remove from heat; stir in parsley and remaining ½ tablespoon lemon juice. Spoon over vegetables and fillets; sprinkle with cheese. Bake at 400° for 15 minutes. Yield: 4 servings.

PER SERVING: 298 CALORIES (17% FROM FAT)
FAT 5.5G (SATURATED FAT 2.1G)
PROTEIN 37.1G CARBOHYDRATE 26.1G
CHOLESTEROL 54MG SODIUM 425MG

SOLE WITH ROASTED GARLIC-POTATO PUREE

2 small heads garlic, unpeeled
Olive oil-flavored vegetable cooking spray
1¼ cups peeled, diced red potato
¼ cup plus 3 tablespoons skim milk
¼ teaspoon salt
¼ teaspoon freshly ground pepper
4 (4-ounce) sole fillets
3 tablespoons freshly grated Parmesan cheese
2 tablespoons fine, dry breadcrumbs
Paprika (optional)
Fresh watercress (optional)

Gently peel outer skin from garlic; cut off top one-fourth of each head, and discard. Place garlic, cut side up, in center of a piece of heavy-duty aluminum foil; coat garlic with cooking spray. Fold aluminum foil over garlic, sealing tightly. Bake at 350° for 1 hour or until garlic is soft. Remove from oven, and let cool.

Remove and discard papery skin from garlic. Scoop out soft garlic, using a small spoon. Set aside soft garlic; discard remaining garlic.

Cook potato in boiling water to cover 15 to 20 minutes or until tender. Drain potato, and mash. Stir in roasted garlic, milk, salt, and pepper. Set aside, and keep warm.

Place fillets in an 11- x 7- x 1½-inch baking dish coated with cooking spray. Combine cheese and breadcrumbs; sprinkle over fillets. Bake, uncovered, at 425° for 12 to 15 minutes or until fish flakes easily when tested with a fork.

Transfer fillets to individual serving plates. Pipe or spoon potato puree evenly onto plates. If desired, sprinkle with paprika, and garnish with fresh watercress. Yield: 4 servings.

PER SERVING: 220 CALORIES (14% FROM FAT)
FAT 3.4G (SATURATED FAT 1.3G)
PROTEIN 26.7G CARBOHYDRATE 19.9G
CHOLESTEROL 64MG SODIUM 367MG

Curried Swordfish with Tropical Fruit Salsa

CURRIED SWORDFISH WITH TROPICAL FRUIT SALSA

1 cup peeled, diced mango
2/3 cup peeled, diced papaya
1/2 cup peeled, seeded, and diced cucumber
1/2 cup seeded, diced plum tomato
1/3 cup diced sweet red pepper
1/3 cup chopped purple onion
3 tablespoons chopped fresh cilantro
2½ tablespoons seeded, finely chopped
    jalapeño pepper
1 tablespoon fresh lemon juice
1/4 teaspoon salt
4 (6-ounce) swordfish steaks (about 1 inch
    thick)
1/4 cup fresh lemon juice
1 tablespoon plus 1 teaspoon curry powder
1 teaspoon cumin seeds
1 teaspoon fennel seeds
2 teaspoons vegetable oil
Vegetable cooking spray

Combine first 9 ingredients in a bowl; toss well. Cover salsa, and chill 3 hours.

Sprinkle salt evenly over fish, and place in a large shallow dish. Combine 1/4 cup lemon juice and next 4 ingredients; stir well. Pour juice mixture over fish; cover and marinate in refrigerator 2 hours.

Remove fish from marinade, reserving marinade. Place fish on rack of a broiler pan coated with cooking spray; broil 5½ inches from heat (with electric oven door partially opened) 4 minutes on each side or until fish flakes easily when tested with a fork, basting frequently with reserved marinade. Serve each steak with 3/4 cup salsa. Yield: 4 servings.

PER SERVING: 297 CALORIES (31% FROM FAT)
FAT 10.1G (SATURATED FAT 2.4G)
PROTEIN 35.3G CARBOHYDRATE 16.7G
CHOLESTEROL 66MG SODIUM 309MG

TILAPIA WITH CORIANDER SHRIMP SAUCE

2/3 cup canned no-salt-added chicken broth,
    undiluted
1/4 cup clam juice
1/2 pound unpeeled small fresh shrimp
1/4 cup dry sherry
1 teaspoon coriander seeds, crushed
1/8 teaspoon pepper
1/4 cup water
2 tablespoons all-purpose flour
4 (4-ounce) tilapia fillets
Fresh cilantro sprigs (optional)

Bring chicken broth and clam juice to a boil in a small saucepan. Add shrimp, and cook 3 to 5 minutes or until shrimp turn pink. Remove shrimp from liquid, using a slotted spoon; reserve liquid. Rinse shrimp with cold water.

Finely chop half of shrimp. (Do not remove shells.) Reserve remaining shrimp. Add finely chopped shrimp, sherry, coriander seeds, and pepper to reserved liquid. Bring to a boil; reduce heat, and simmer, uncovered, 15 minutes or until reduced to 3/4 cup. Pour mixture through a wire-mesh strainer into a bowl, discarding solids. Return liquid to pan.

Peel, devein, and chop reserved shrimp; set shrimp aside.

Combine water and flour, stirring until smooth. Stir into liquid mixture. Cook, stirring constantly, until thickened and bubbly. Add peeled chopped shrimp; stir well.

Place fillets in a 13- x 9- x 2-inch baking dish; pour shrimp mixture over fillets. Bake, uncovered, at 450° for 10 minutes or until fish flakes easily when tested with a fork.

Transfer fillets to a serving platter; spoon sauce over fillets. Garnish with fresh cilantro sprigs, if desired. Yield: 4 servings.

PER SERVING: 156 CALORIES (20% FROM FAT)
FAT 3.5G (SATURATED FAT 0.6G)
PROTEIN 26.2G CARBOHYDRATE 3.7G
CHOLESTEROL 112MG SODIUM 146MG

Sautéed Trout with Corn Relish

SAUTÉED TROUT WITH CORN RELISH

½ cup diced sweet red pepper
1 tablespoon brown sugar
2 tablespoons minced fresh onion
2 tablespoons red wine vinegar
¼ teaspoon salt
¼ teaspoon ground cumin
⅛ teaspoon dried crushed red pepper
1 cup fresh corn cut from cob or 1 (7-ounce)
    can whole-kernel corn, drained
2 tablespoons cornmeal
¼ teaspoon chili powder
⅛ teaspoon salt
2 (6-ounce) speckled trout fillets
2 teaspoons vegetable oil
Lemon rind strips (optional)
Fresh chives (optional)

Combine first 7 ingredients in a large nonstick skillet; stir well. Place skillet over medium heat, and cook 5 minutes, stirring frequently. Add corn; cook 2 minutes, stirring frequently. Spoon relish into a bowl; set aside, and keep warm. Wipe skillet clean with a paper towel.

Combine cornmeal, chili powder, and ⅛ teaspoon salt in a shallow dish; stir well. Dredge fillets in cornmeal mixture. Heat oil in skillet over medium heat. Add fillets to skillet, and cook 3 minutes on each side or until fish flakes easily when tested with a fork. Serve each fillet with about ½ cup relish. If desired, garnish with lemon rind and chives. Yield: 2 servings.

PER SERVING: 438 CALORIES (27% FROM FAT)
FAT 13.2G (SATURATED FAT 2.4G)
PROTEIN 48.6G   CARBOHYDRATE 31.8G
CHOLESTEROL 124MG   SODIUM 517MG

TUNA WITH ROASTED TOMATO AND BEANS

1 cup coarsely chopped plum tomato
½ cup coarsely chopped onion
2 teaspoons olive oil
2 cloves garlic, slivered
1 (15-ounce) can cannellini beans, drained
¼ cup chopped fresh parsley
1 teaspoon chopped fresh oregano
1 teaspoon red wine vinegar
½ teaspoon chopped fresh thyme
¼ teaspoon freshly ground pepper
⅛ teaspoon salt
1 tablespoon red wine vinegar
2 teaspoons olive oil
⅛ teaspoon freshly ground pepper
4 (4-ounce) tuna steaks
Vegetable cooking spray
Fresh oregano sprigs (optional)
Fresh thyme sprigs (optional)

Combine first 4 ingredients in a small bowl; spoon tomato mixture into an 11- x 7- x 1½-inch baking dish. Bake, uncovered, at 425° for 25 minutes or until tomato liquid evaporates and onion is tender. Add beans and next 6 ingredients; cover and bake 10 minutes or until thoroughly heated. Remove bean mixture from oven. Set aside, and keep warm.

Combine 1 tablespoon red wine vinegar, 2 teaspoons olive oil, and ⅛ teaspoon pepper in a small bowl, stirring well. Brush vinegar mixture evenly over both sides of tuna steaks.

Place tuna steaks on rack of a broiler pan coated with cooking spray. Broil 5½ inches from heat (with electric oven door partially opened) 5 minutes on each side or until fish flakes easily when tested with a fork.

Transfer tuna steaks to a serving platter; spoon bean mixture evenly over steaks. If desired, garnish with fresh oregano and thyme sprigs. Yield: 4 servings.

PER SERVING: 312 CALORIES (30% FROM FAT)
FAT 10.5G (SATURATED FAT 2.1G)
PROTEIN 32.6G CARBOHYDRATE 22.0G
CHOLESTEROL 42MG SODIUM 244MG

SEARED TUNA PROVENÇAL

Olive oil-flavored vegetable cooking spray
2 teaspoons minced garlic
1 cup thinly sliced sweet red pepper
1 cup thinly sliced sweet yellow pepper
¾ cup thinly sliced purple onion
1½ cups peeled, seeded, and chopped tomato
¼ cup dry red wine
½ teaspoon dried rosemary
½ teaspoon freshly ground pepper
¼ teaspoon salt
4 (4-ounce) tuna steaks (1 inch thick)
1 teaspoon olive oil

Coat a large nonstick skillet with cooking spray; place over medium-high heat until hot. Add garlic, and sauté 1 minute. Add sweet peppers and onion; sauté until tender. Add tomato, wine, and rosemary; bring to a boil. Reduce heat, and simmer, uncovered, 10 minutes or until vegetables are tender, stirring occasionally. Stir in pepper and salt. Set aside, and keep warm.

Brush both sides of each steak with olive oil. Coat a large cast-iron skillet with cooking spray. Place over high heat until almost smoking. Add tuna steaks, and sear 45 seconds to 1 minute on each side or until browned. Immediately place skillet in oven, and bake at 400° for 8 to 10 minutes or until fish flakes easily then tested with a fork. Transfer steaks to a serving platter. To serve, spoon vegetable mixture evenly over steaks. Yield: 4 servings.

PER SERVING: 219 CALORIES (30% FROM FAT)
FAT 7.4G (SATURATED FAT 1.7G)
PROTEIN 28.1G CARBOHYDRATE 10.0G
CHOLESTEROL 43MG SODIUM 202MG

Scallop-Vegetable Sauté (recipe on page 97)

SHELLFISH: PLAIN & FANCY

The beauty of lobster, shrimp, and other shellfish is that they taste great in the simplest dishes. Take Boiled Lobster, for example—it's a real delight, either unadorned or served with a sauce. If you've never prepared live lobster, just turn to page 95 to see how it's done. It's easier than you think.

Although shellfish is naturally low in fat, many of the classic dishes call for heavy doses of butter or oil. But not a drop of either is used in Shrimp Creole (page 104). As a result, only 7 percent of its calories are from fat. Rich-tasting Seafood Newberg (page 92) calls for a low-fat white sauce instead of cream to keep the calories and fat low.

In this chapter you'll also find recipes for clams, crabmeat, mussels, and oysters. Be sure to try Mussels Marinara (page 96) right away—it was a favorite when taste-tested.

Linguine with Clam Sauce

LINGUINE WITH CLAM SAUCE

36 small fresh clams (about 2 pounds)
2 tablespoons cornmeal
2 teaspoons olive oil
3 tablespoons chopped shallots
1½ cups dry white wine
⅓ cup minced fresh flat-leaf parsley
½ teaspoon salt
¼ to ½ teaspoon dried crushed red pepper
¼ teaspoon black pepper
8 cloves garlic, minced
8 cups cooked linguine (about 16 ounces
    uncooked), cooked without salt or fat
4 lemon wedges
Parsley sprigs (optional)

Scrub clam shells with a brush, discarding any that are cracked or open. Place clams in a large bowl; cover with cold water. Sprinkle with cornmeal; let stand 30 minutes. Drain and rinse clams, discarding cornmeal; set aside.

Heat oil in a large nonstick skillet over medium-high heat. Add shallots; sauté 2 minutes. Add wine and next 5 ingredients; bring to a boil. Add clams; cover, reduce heat, and simmer 5 minutes or until shells open. Discard any unopened shells. Remove clams with a slotted spoon; set aside.

Place 2 cups pasta in each of 4 shallow bowls; spoon ½ cup wine sauce over each, and top with clams. Serve with lemon wedges; garnish with parsley sprigs, if desired. Yield: 4 servings.

PER SERVING: 429 CALORIES (9% FROM FAT)
FAT 4.4G (SATURATED FAT 0.6G)
PROTEIN 16.4G   CARBOHYDRATE 82.1G
CHOLESTEROL 7MG   SODIUM 321MG

Clams in Lemon White Sauce

4 pounds littleneck clams (about 20 clams)
3 tablespoons cornmeal
1 cup chopped onion
2 tablespoons chopped shallots
1½ cups dry white wine
2 tablespoons reduced-calorie margarine
2 tablespoons all-purpose flour
1 cup 1% low-fat milk
2 teaspoons grated lemon rind
¼ cup fresh lemon juice
2 cloves garlic, minced
2 tablespoons minced fresh parsley
2 tablespoons minced green onions
¼ teaspoon salt
¼ teaspoon ground white pepper

Scrub clam shells with a brush, discarding any that are cracked or open. Place clams in a large bowl; cover with cold water, and sprinkle with cornmeal. Let stand 30 minutes. Drain and rinse clams, discarding cornmeal; set aside.

Combine clams, chopped onion, shallots, and wine in a large Dutch oven. Bring to a boil; cover, reduce heat, and simmer 6 minutes or until most clams are open. Remove clams to a serving bowl as they open; keep warm. Discard any unopened clams. Bring remaining liquid to a boil; cook over high heat until reduced to 1 cup. Pour liquid through a sieve, and set aside.

Melt margarine in a heavy saucepan over low heat; add flour, stirring until smooth. Cook, stirring constantly, 1 minute. Gradually add milk, reserved 1 cup clam liquid, lemon rind, lemon juice, and garlic. Cook over medium heat, stirring constantly, until mixture is thickened and bubbly. Remove from heat; stir in parsley, green onions, salt, and pepper. To serve, pour sauce over clams. Yield: 2 servings.

PER SERVING: 265 CALORIES (33% FROM FAT)
FAT 9.7G (SATURATED FAT 1.9G)
PROTEIN 18.6G CARBOHYDRATE 28.3G
CHOLESTEROL 37MG SODIUM 537MG

Maryland Silver Queen Crab Cakes

1¼ cups fresh Silver Queen corn cut from the cob (about 2 ears)
1 egg white
1 pound fresh lump crabmeat, drained
¼ cup plus 2 tablespoons fine, dry breadcrumbs
1 tablespoon dried parsley flakes
1 tablespoon low-sodium Worcestershire sauce
1 teaspoon Dijon mustard
¼ teaspoon Old Bay seasoning
Vegetable cooking spray

Position knife blade in food processor bowl; add corn. Process 8 seconds, scraping sides of processor bowl once. Add egg white; process 2 seconds. Transfer mixture to a bowl; stir in crabmeat and next 5 ingredients. Cover; chill at least 30 minutes.

Shape mixture into 6 patties. Place on a baking sheet coated with cooking spray. Broil 5½ inches from heat (with electric oven door partially opened) 10 minutes on each side. Yield: 6 servings.

PER SERVING: 137 CALORIES (14% FROM FAT)
FAT 2.1G (SATURATED FAT 0.3G)
PROTEIN 16.7G CARBOHYDRATE 13.0G
CHOLESTEROL 71MG SODIUM 316MG

Before shucking clams, scrub them thoroughly under cool running water. Cover clams with water; add 2 to 3 tablespoons of cornmeal. Wait 30 minutes for clams to eat the meal and rid themselves of sand and grit. Drain and rinse clams.

Crabmeat Imperial

CRABMEAT IMPERIAL

Vegetable cooking spray
¼ cup chopped celery
¼ cup chopped green pepper
¼ cup chopped sweet red pepper
1 egg, lightly beaten
¼ cup plus 1 tablespoon nonfat mayonnaise,
    divided
1 tablespoon chopped fresh parsley
1½ tablespoons lemon juice
1½ tablespoons low-sodium soy sauce
½ teaspoon Dijon mustard
⅛ teaspoon ground red pepper
⅛ teaspoon hot sauce
1 pound fresh lump crabmeat, drained
Pimiento strips (optional)
Celery leaves (optional)

Coat a small nonstick skillet with cooking spray;
place over medium-high heat until hot. Add celery,
green pepper, and sweet red pepper; sauté until
tender. Combine egg and 3 tablespoons mayonnaise
in a medium bowl; add pepper mixture, parsley,
and next 5 ingredients, stirring well. Add crabmeat;
stir gently just until blended.

Spoon crabmeat mixture evenly into 4 baking
shells. Place shells on a baking sheet. Bake at 375°
for 20 minutes or until golden. Remove from oven,
and top evenly with remaining 2 tablespoons mayonnaise. If desired, garnish with pimiento strips
and celery leaves. Yield: 4 servings.

PER SERVING: 149 CALORIES (21% FROM FAT)
FAT 3.5G (SATURATED FAT 0.7G)
PROTEIN 24.0G CARBOHYDRATE 3.7G
CHOLESTEROL 165MG SODIUM 541MG

CHEESY CRABMEAT BAKE

Vegetable cooking spray
1 tablespoon reduced-calorie margarine
1¼ cups canned no-salt-added chicken broth,
    undiluted and divided
½ pound fresh mushrooms, quartered
1 pound fresh lump crabmeat, drained
¼ teaspoon salt
¼ teaspoon ground white pepper
¼ cup plus 2 tablespoons all-purpose flour
¾ cup 1% low-fat milk, divided
½ cup nonfat sour cream
¼ cup (1 ounce) finely shredded reduced-fat
    Swiss cheese
1 tablespoon lemon juice
1 teaspoon minced garlic
1 (14-ounce) can artichoke hearts, drained and
    quartered
2 tablespoons fine, dry breadcrumbs
2 tablespoons freshly grated Parmesan cheese
2 teaspoons reduced-calorie margarine, melted
½ teaspoon paprika

Coat a large nonstick skillet with cooking spray;
add 1 tablespoon margarine. Place over medium-
high heat until margarine melts. Add ½ cup broth
and mushrooms; cook over high heat until liquid
evaporates. Remove from heat; stir in crabmeat,
salt, and pepper.

Combine flour and ¼ cup milk, mixing well.
Combine remaining ½ cup milk and remaining ¾
cup broth in a saucepan; add flour mixture. Cook
over medium heat, stirring constantly, until thickened. Remove from heat; stir in sour cream and
next 3 ingredients. Stir in crabmeat mixture and
artichokes. Spoon into a shallow 2-quart baking
dish coated with cooking spray.

Combine breadcrumbs, Parmesan cheese, 2 teaspoons margarine, and paprika. Sprinkle over
crabmeat mixture. Bake, uncovered, at 400° for 15
minutes or until lightly browned. Yield: 6 servings.

PER SERVING: 212 CALORIES (24% FROM FAT)
FAT 5.6G (SATURATED FAT 1.6G)
PROTEIN 22.0G CARBOHYDRATE 17.5G
CHOLESTEROL 77MG SODIUM 447MG

CRABMEAT CRÊPES

12 very thin asparagus spears
1 tablespoon plus 1½ teaspoons all-purpose
    flour
½ cup 1% low-fat milk, divided
2 tablespoons instant nonfat dry milk powder
1½ teaspoons reduced-calorie margarine
¼ pound fresh lump crabmeat, drained
1 tablespoon chopped green onions
2½ teaspoons chopped fresh thyme
1½ teaspoons chopped fresh parsley
2 teaspoons dry sherry
½ teaspoon lemon juice
⅛ teaspoon salt
⅛ teaspoon ground red pepper
4 Crêpes

Snap off tough ends of asparagus. Remove scales
from stalks with a knife or vegetable peeler, if
desired. Arrange asparagus in a steamer basket over
boiling water. Cover and steam 4 to 5 minutes or
until crisp-tender.

Combine flour and 1 tablespoon milk, stirring
until smooth. Combine flour mixture, remaining ¼
cup plus 3 tablespoons milk, milk powder, and
margarine in a small saucepan, stirring well. Cook
over medium heat, stirring constantly, until mixture
is thickened and bubbly. Remove from heat; stir in
crabmeat and next 7 ingredients. Reserve ¼ cup
crabmeat mixture.

Arrange 3 asparagus spears in center of each
Crêpe. Spoon remaining crabmeat mixture evenly
over asparagus. Roll up Crêpes, and place, seam
side down, in an 11- x 7- x 1½-inch baking dish.
Top with reserved crabmeat mixture. Cover and
bake at 350° for 15 minutes. Yield: 2 servings.

CRÊPES
¼ cup all-purpose flour
⅓ cup 1% low-fat milk
2 tablespoons frozen egg substitute, thawed
¼ teaspoon vegetable oil
Vegetable cooking spray

Combine first 4 ingredients, stirring just until
smooth. Chill at least 1 hour.

Coat a 6-inch crêpe pan or nonstick skillet with

cooking spray; place over medium heat until hot.
Pour 2 tablespoons batter into pan; quickly tilt pan
in all directions so batter covers pan in a thin film.
Cook 1 minute or until crêpe can be shaken loose
from pan. Flip crêpe, and cook about 30 seconds.

Place crêpe on a towel to cool. Repeat until all
batter is used. Stack crêpes between layers of wax
paper to prevent sticking. Yield: 4 (6-inch) crêpes.

PER SERVING: 254 CALORIES (18% FROM FAT)
FAT 5.2G (SATURATED FAT 1.3G)
PROTEIN 22.8G   CARBOHYDRATE 29.0G
CHOLESTEROL 62MG   SODIUM 443MG

SEAFOOD NEWBURG

2 (8-ounce) fresh or frozen lobster tails,
    thawed
3 ounces Neufchâtel cheese
Vegetable cooking spray
1 teaspoon vegetable oil
⅔ cup sliced fresh mushrooms
½ cup chopped onion
⅓ cup all-purpose flour
3 cups skim milk
2 tablespoons frozen egg substitute, thawed
3 tablespoons dry sherry
1 tablespoon lemon juice
¼ teaspoon salt
¼ teaspoon black pepper
⅛ teaspoon dry mustard
⅛ teaspoon paprika
Dash of ground red pepper
½ pound fresh lump crabmeat, drained
6 cups cooked long-grain rice (cooked without
    salt or fat)
Paprika
Parsley sprigs (optional)
Lemon slices (optional)

Cook lobster tails in boiling water 6 to 8 minutes
or until done; drain. Rinse tails with cold water.
Split and clean tails. Coarsely chop meat; set aside.

Freeze cheese 15 minutes or until firm; cut
cheese into ¼-inch cubes, and set aside.

Coat a large nonstick skillet with cooking spray;
add oil. Place over medium heat until hot. Add

Seafood Newburg

mushrooms and onion; sauté until tender. Add flour; cook, stirring constantly, 1 minute.

Combine milk and egg substitute; stir well. Gradually add milk mixture to flour mixture; cook, stirring constantly, until mixture is thickened.

Add cheese, stirring until cheese melts. Stir in lobster, sherry, and next 7 ingredients; cook, stirring constantly, 2 to 3 minutes or until thoroughly heated. Place 1 cup rice on each individual plate. Top with equal amounts of seafood mixture, and sprinkle with paprika. If desired, garnish with parsley and lemon slices. Yield: 6 servings.

PER SERVING: 305 CALORIES (17% FROM FAT)
FAT 5.7G (SATURATED FAT 2.6G)
PROTEIN 26.4G   CARBOHYDRATE 35.3G
CHOLESTEROL 100MG   SODIUM 333MG

Lobster with Light Curry Sauce

LOBSTER WITH LIGHT CURRY SAUCE

2 (8-ounce) fresh or frozen lobster tails, thawed
Vegetable cooking spray
1 tablespoon margarine
2 teaspoons curry powder
1 tablespoon peeled, minced gingerroot
1 teaspoon minced garlic
½ cup evaporated skimmed milk
½ cup clam juice
¼ cup dry white wine
¼ cup ruby port wine
1 tablespoon balsamic vinegar
¼ teaspoon freshly ground black pepper
¼ teaspoon dried crushed red pepper
Sliced green onions (optional)

Cut lobster tails in half lengthwise, cutting through upper and lower hard shells with an electric knife. Coat a large nonstick skillet with cooking spray; place over medium-high heat until hot. Add lobster tail halves, cut side down. Cook 4 minutes on each side or until lobster is done. Remove lobster from skillet, and keep warm.

Add margarine and curry powder to skillet; heat over medium-high heat until margarine melts. Cook 30 seconds over medium-high heat, stirring constantly. Add gingerroot and garlic, and sauté until tender. Add milk and next 6 ingredients; stir well. Cook over medium-high heat, stirring constantly, 10 to 12 minutes or until mixture is reduced to ½ cup.

Spoon ¼ cup curry mixture onto each individual serving plate. Place 2 lobster tail halves, cut side down, on each plate. Garnish with green onions, if desired. Yield: 2 servings.

PER SERVING: 274 CALORIES (26% FROM FAT)
FAT 7.9G (SATURATED FAT 1.6G)
PROTEIN 38.0G   CARBOHYDRATE 11.6G
CHOLESTEROL 165MG   SODIUM 581MG

BOILED LOBSTER

2 tablespoons salt
2 fresh lobsters

Fill an 8-quart Dutch oven two-thirds full with water; add salt, and bring to a rapid boil over high heat. Using tongs, plunge lobsters headfirst into the water; return to a boil. Cover, reduce heat, and simmer 8 minutes for smaller lobsters (1 to 1¼ pounds) and 10 minutes for larger lobsters (1½ to 2 pounds). If desired, serve with Herb Sauce or Creamy Cocktail Sauce. Yield: 2 servings.

PER SERVING: 90 CALORIES (9% FROM FAT)
FAT 0.9G (SATURATED FAT 0.2G)
PROTEIN 18.8G   CARBOHYDRATE 0.5G
CHOLESTEROL 95MG   SODIUM 963MG

HERB SAUCE

This healthy alternative to clarified butter has about half the fat grams per tablespoon.

½ cup reduced-calorie margarine, melted
1 tablespoon finely chopped fresh basil
1 clove garlic, crushed

Combine all ingredients in a bowl; stir well. Serve with fish or shellfish. Yield: ½ cup.

PER TABLESPOON: 51 CALORIES (99% FROM FAT)
FAT 5.6G (SATURATED FAT 0.9G)
PROTEIN 0.1G   CARBOHYDRATE 0.2G
CHOLESTEROL 0MG   SODIUM 139MG

CREAMY COCKTAIL SAUCE

½ cup plain low-fat yogurt
½ cup reduced-fat mayonnaise
2 tablespoons seafood cocktail sauce

Combine all ingredients; cover and chill. Serve with fish or shellfish. Yield: 1 cup plus 2 tablespoons.

PER TABLESPOON: 24 CALORIES (71% FROM FAT)
FAT 1.9G (SATURATED FAT 0.3G)
PROTEIN 0.4G   CARBOHYDRATE 1.3G
CHOLESTEROL 3MG   SODIUM 74MG

MUSSELS MARINARA

5   pounds fresh mussels (about 100 mussels)
1   tablespoon olive oil
1   cup finely chopped onion
3   cloves garlic, minced
2   cups chopped tomato
½   cup dry white wine
⅓   cup chopped fresh flat-leaf parsley
2   tablespoons chopped fresh basil
½   teaspoon salt
½   teaspoon black pepper
¼   teaspoon dried crushed red pepper
2   bay leaves
5   cups cooked linguine (about 10 ounces
      uncooked), cooked without salt or fat
Basil sprigs (optional)

Remove beards on mussels; scrub shells with a brush. Discard open, cracked, or heavy mussels (they're filled with sand). Set aside remaining mussels.

Heat oil in a large stockpot over medium-high heat. Add onion and garlic; sauté 3 minutes. Add tomato and next 7 ingredients; cook over medium heat 5 minutes. Add mussels; cover and cook 10 minutes or until mussels open. Discard bay leaves and any unopened shells.

Place 1 cup linguine in each of 5 individual shallow bowls. Remove mussels with a slotted spoon, and divide among bowls. Spoon about ½ cup tomato mixture into each bowl. Garnish with basil sprigs, if desired. Yield: 5 servings.

PER SERVING: 305 CALORIES (17% FROM FAT)
FAT 5.6G (SATURATED FAT 0.9G)
PROTEIN 16.0G   CARBOHYDRATE 47.6G
CHOLESTEROL 20MG   SODIUM 451MG

Mussels Marinara

OYSTERS FLORENTINE

1 pound fresh spinach
Vegetable cooking spray
2 tablespoons minced shallots
1 clove garlic, minced
¼ teaspoon pepper, divided
½ cup clam juice, divided
1½ teaspoons cornstarch
1½ teaspoons lemon juice
1½ teaspoons minced garlic, divided
¼ cup fine, dry breadcrumbs
¼ cup grated Parmesan cheese
1 tablespoon reduced-calorie margarine,
    melted
36 oysters on the half shell
1 (4-pound) package rock salt

Remove and discard stems from spinach. Wash leaves; pat dry. Coat a nonstick skillet with cooking spray; place over medium-high heat until hot. Add one-third of spinach; sauté 1 minute or until wilted. Set aside. Repeat procedure twice. Chop spinach.

Coat skillet with cooking spray; place over medium-high heat until hot. Add shallots and 1 minced clove garlic; sauté until tender. Stir in spinach and ⅛ teaspoon pepper.

Combine 1 tablespoon clam juice and cornstarch; set aside. Combine remaining ¼ cup plus 3 tablespoons clam juice, lemon juice, and ½ teaspoon garlic in a saucepan; bring to a boil. Reduce heat; simmer 1 minute. Stir in cornstarch mixture. Cook, stirring constantly, until thickened. Stir in remaining ⅛ teaspoon pepper. Combine remaining 1 teaspoon garlic, breadcrumbs, cheese, and margarine.

Scrape a knife between oysters and shells to free meat, and set shells aside. Place oysters in a colander to drain.

Sprinkle rock salt in two 15- x 10- x 1-inch jelly-roll pans; arrange reserved shells on salt. Place 1 oyster in each half shell. Top with spinach mixture; drizzle with sauce. Sprinkle with breadcrumb mixture. Broil 3 inches from heat (with electric oven door partially opened) 4 minutes. Yield: 6 servings.

PER SERVING: 123 CALORIES (35% FROM FAT)
FAT 4.8G (SATURATED FAT 1.4G)
PROTEIN 10.3G   CARBOHYDRATE 10.4G
CHOLESTEROL 50MG   SODIUM 309MG

SCALLOP-VEGETABLE SAUTÉ

(pictured on page 86)

Vegetable cooking spray
2 teaspoons olive oil
1 pound fresh Sugar Snap peas
2 cups diagonally sliced celery
1 tablespoon minced fresh chives
2 cloves garlic
1 pound fresh sea scallops
⅓ cup vermouth or dry white wine
1½ teaspoons grated lemon rind
3 tablespoons lemon juice
½ teaspoon dried oregano
½ teaspoon chicken-flavored bouillon granules
½ teaspoon pepper
2 tablespoons chopped fresh parsley

Coat a large nonstick skillet with cooking spray; add oil. Place over medium-high heat until hot. Add peas, celery, chives, and garlic; sauté 3 to 4 minutes or until crisp-tender. Remove vegetables from skillet, using a slotted spoon; set aside, and keep warm.

Add scallops and next 6 ingredients to skillet; bring to a boil. Cover, reduce heat, and simmer 6 minutes or until scallops are opaque. Remove scallops from skillet, using a slotted spoon; set aside, and keep warm. Cook liquid in skillet until reduced to about 1 tablespoon. Return scallops and vegetables to skillet, and cook, stirring constantly, just until thoroughly heated; add chopped parsley, and toss. Yield: 4 servings.

PER SERVING: 193 CALORIES (19% FROM FAT)
FAT 4.0G (SATURATED FAT 0.6G)
PROTEIN 23.0G   CARBOHYDRATE 16.6G
CHOLESTEROL 37MG   SODIUM 459MG

SCALLOPS WITH VEGETABLE-CREAM SAUCE

Olive oil-flavored vegetable cooking spray
2 tablespoons chopped shallots
2 teaspoons minced garlic
2⅓ cups sliced fresh mushrooms
⅓ cup skim milk
2 ounces Neufchâtel cheese
¼ teaspoon salt
½ teaspoon olive oil
18 ounces sea scallops, cut in half
1½ tablespoons all-purpose flour
⅓ cup dry vermouth
2 tablespoons clam juice
1½ cups thinly sliced fresh spinach
1 teaspoon fresh lemon juice
¼ teaspoon ground white pepper
¼ cup plus 2 tablespoons (1½ ounces) shredded Gruyère cheese

Coat a medium-size nonstick skillet with cooking spray. Place over medium-high heat until hot. Add shallots and garlic, and sauté 1 minute. Add mushrooms; sauté 2 minutes. Add milk, Neufchâtel cheese, and salt; cook, stirring constantly, until cheese melts. Remove from heat; set aside.

Coat a large nonstick skillet with cooking spray; add oil. Place over medium-high heat until hot. Add scallops; cook 3 to 4 minutes or until scallops are lightly browned, turning to brown all sides. Combine flour, vermouth, and clam juice, stirring until smooth. Add vermouth mixture, mushroom mixture, and spinach to scallops. Bring to a boil; reduce heat, and simmer, uncovered, 4 minutes. Remove from heat; stir in lemon juice and pepper.

Spoon scallop mixture evenly into 6 baking shells; sprinkle evenly with Gruyère cheese. Broil 5½ inches from heat (with electric oven door partially opened) 3 to 4 minutes or until lightly browned. Yield: 6 servings.

PER SERVING: 167 CALORIES (33% FROM FAT)
FAT 6.2G (SATURATED FAT 2.9G)
PROTEIN 19.2G   CARBOHYDRATE 8.3G
CHOLESTEROL 43MG   SODIUM 323MG

SCALLOPS IN CREAMY TARRAGON SAUCE

4 ounces spinach fettuccine, uncooked
Vegetable cooking spray
1½ cups sliced fresh mushrooms
2 tablespoons sliced green onions
1 clove garlic, minced
1 pound bay scallops
⅓ cup dry white wine
1½ tablespoons lemon juice
1½ teaspoons chopped fresh tarragon or ½ teaspoon dried tarragon
1 tablespoon reduced-calorie margarine
1½ tablespoons all-purpose flour
¼ teaspoon salt
⅓ cup nonfat sour cream
Chopped fresh parsley (optional)

Cook spinach fettuccine according to package directions, omitting salt and fat. Drain; set aside, and keep warm.

Coat a large skillet with cooking spray; place over medium-high heat until hot. Add mushrooms, green onions, and garlic; sauté 1 to 2 minutes or until vegetables are tender.

Add scallops, wine, lemon juice, and tarragon to mushroom mixture. Bring to a boil over medium-high heat. Reduce heat to low, and cook 4 minutes or until scallops are opaque. Remove scallops and vegetables from skillet, using a slotted spoon; set aside.

Simmer wine mixture, uncovered, 5 minutes or until reduced to ¾ cup. Remove from heat; set aside.

Melt margarine in a small, heavy saucepan over medium heat; add flour and salt. Cook, stirring constantly with a wire whisk, 1 minute. Gradually add reserved wine mixture, stirring constantly. Cook, stirring constantly, until thickened and bubbly. Remove from heat, and let cool 1 minute. Stir in scallop mixture and sour cream.

Place fettuccine on a serving platter. Spoon scallop mixture over fettuccine; garnish with chopped parsley, if desired. Yield: 4 servings.

PER SERVING: 260 CALORIES (15% FROM FAT)
FAT 4.3G (SATURATED FAT 0.7G)
PROTEIN 25.6G   CARBOHYDRATE 28.7G
CHOLESTEROL 65MG   SODIUM 394MG

Scallops in Creamy Tarragon Sauce

Sautéed Scallops on Lemon Fettuccine

SAUTÉED SCALLOPS ON LEMON FETTUCCINE

¼ cup all-purpose flour
½ teaspoon salt
½ teaspoon cracked pepper
1 pound sea scallops
2 teaspoons olive oil
2 teaspoons margarine
⅓ cup vodka or dry white wine
1 teaspoon grated lemon rind
3 tablespoons fresh lemon juice
1 clove garlic, minced
6 cups cooked fettuccine (about 12 ounces
    uncooked), cooked without salt or fat
¼ cup freshly grated Parmesan cheese
¼ cup chopped fresh flat-leaf parsley

Combine first 3 ingredients in a large heavy-duty, zip-top plastic bag. Add scallops to bag; seal bag, and shake to coat.

Heat oil and margarine in a large nonstick skillet over high heat. Add scallops; cook 2 minutes on each side or until scallops are opaque and lightly browned. Remove scallops from pan, and keep warm; reduce heat to medium. Add vodka, lemon rind, lemon juice, and garlic; cook 3 minutes, stirring occasionally. Remove from heat; add pasta, and toss gently to coat.

Divide pasta mixture evenly among 4 individual plates; top with scallops. Sprinkle each serving with 1 tablespoon cheese and 1 tablespoon parsley. Yield: 4 servings.

PER SERVING: 481 CALORIES (14% FROM FAT)
FAT 7.3G (SATURATED FAT 1.6G)
PROTEIN 30.6G   CARBOHYDRATE 65.3G
CHOLESTEROL 40MG   SODIUM 559MG

SCALLOP, MUSHROOM, AND ASPARAGUS ROLLS

6 ounces fresh asparagus
Butter-flavored vegetable cooking spray
2⅔ cups chopped fresh mushrooms
¼ cup chopped shallots
½ pound bay scallops
½ cup light process cream cheese
1 teaspoon freshly ground pepper
4 sheets commercial frozen phyllo pastry,
    thawed
2 tablespoons plus 2 teaspoons fine, dry
    breadcrumbs
1 teaspoon reduced-calorie margarine, melted

Snap off tough ends of asparagus. Remove scales from stalks with a knife or vegetable peeler, if desired. Coarsely chop asparagus. Arrange asparagus in a steamer basket over boiling water. Cover and steam 3 minutes or until crisp-tender. Drain and set aside.

Coat a large nonstick skillet with cooking spray. Place over medium-high heat until hot. Add mushrooms and shallots; sauté 4 minutes. Add scallops, and cook, stirring constantly, 2 minutes. Stir in asparagus, cream cheese, and pepper; cook, stirring constantly, 5 to 6 minutes or until mixture thickens. Remove from heat, and set aside.

Place 1 sheet of phyllo on a damp towel (keep remaining phyllo covered). Lightly coat phyllo with cooking spray, and sprinkle with 2 teaspoons breadcrumbs. Top with 1 sheet of phyllo; sprinkle with 2 teaspoons breadcrumbs. Fold phyllo in half crosswise.

Spoon half of scallop mixture along one lengthwise edge of phyllo, leaving a 1-inch border on short edges. Fold short edges in about 1 inch, and roll up, jellyroll fashion, starting with long side containing scallop mixture.

Place roll, seam side down, on a baking sheet coated with cooking spray. Lightly coat top of pastry with cooking spray. Repeat procedure with remaining phyllo, breadcrumbs, and scallop mixture. Brush melted margarine evenly over rolls.

Bake at 400° for 15 minutes or until crisp and golden. Remove from oven, and cut each roll into fourths. Serve immediately. Yield: 4 servings.

PER SERVING: 234 CALORIES (32% FROM FAT)
FAT 8.3G (SATURATED FAT 3.2G)
PROTEIN 16.8G CARBOHYDRATE 23.5G
CHOLESTEROL 35MG SODIUM 410MG

SCALLOPS PESTO

3 tablespoons chopped fresh basil
1 tablespoon chopped fresh parsley
1 teaspoon pine nuts
¼ teaspoon salt
1 large clove garlic
2 teaspoons olive oil
1 cup canned no-salt-added chicken broth,
    undiluted
1 pound sea scallops
2 tablespoons all-purpose flour
3 tablespoons water
5 ounces fettuccine, uncooked
Fresh basil sprigs (optional)
Fresh parsley sprigs (optional)

Combine first 5 ingredients in a coffee grinder or miniature food processor; process until finely chopped. Add olive oil; process until smooth.

Bring broth to a boil in a large nonstick skillet. Reduce heat, and add scallops; cover and simmer 4 minutes or until scallops are opaque. Remove scallops from broth; set aside. Cook broth, uncovered, over medium heat until reduced to ½ cup.

Combine flour and water, stirring well. Add to broth, stirring well. Cook over medium heat, stirring constantly, until thickened and bubbly. Stir in herb mixture and scallops; cook until heated.

Cook pasta according to package directions, omitting salt and fat; drain. Combine pasta and scallop mixture in a bowl; toss. If desired, garnish with fresh basil and parsley sprigs. Yield: 4 servings.

PER SERVING: 285 CALORIES (17% FROM FAT)
FAT 5.3G (SATURATED FAT 0.7G)
PROTEIN 24.8G CARBOHYDRATE 32.9G
CHOLESTEROL 37MG SODIUM 367MG

SHRIMP CURRY

1¼ pounds unpeeled medium-size fresh
    shrimp
6 cups water
Vegetable cooking spray
2 teaspoons reduced-calorie margarine
½ cup chopped onion
2 tablespoons plus 1 teaspoon all-purpose flour
1 tablespoon curry powder
2 cups skim milk
2 teaspoons lemon juice
¼ teaspoon salt
2 cups cooked long-grain rice (cooked without
    salt or fat)
¼ cup chopped green onions
¼ cup cubed banana
¼ cup raisins
2 tablespoons chopped fresh parsley
1 tablespoon plus 1 teaspoon unsweetened
    coconut

Peel and devein shrimp; set aside.

Bring water to a boil in a large saucepan. Add shrimp; cook 3 to 5 minutes or until shrimp turn pink. Drain well.

Coat a large nonstick skillet with cooking spray; add margarine. Place over medium-high heat until margarine melts. Add ½ cup chopped onion; sauté until tender. Combine flour and curry powder; sprinkle over onion, stirring until blended. Gradually add milk, stirring constantly. Cook, stirring constantly, 10 minutes or until thickened. Add lemon juice and salt; stir well. Add shrimp, and cook until thoroughly heated.

Place rice on a large serving platter. Spoon shrimp mixture over rice; top evenly with green onions and remaining ingredients. Yield: 4 servings.

PER SERVING: 345 CALORIES (11% FROM FAT)
FAT 4.2G (SATURATED FAT 1.6G)
PROTEIN 25.1G CARBOHYDRATE 51.4G
CHOLESTEROL 158MG SODIUM 414MG

POLYNESIAN SHRIMP

Served on a bed of steamed rice, this traditional stir-fry is made entirely in the microwave.

1 pound unpeeled medium-size fresh shrimp
1 cup julienne-sliced green pepper
1 cup julienne-sliced sweet red pepper
1 cup thinly sliced onion, separated into rings
1 (20-ounce) can unsweetened pineapple
    chunks, undrained
¼ cup firmly packed brown sugar
1 tablespoon plus 2 teaspoons cornstarch
1 teaspoon peeled, grated gingerroot
¼ teaspoon salt
¼ cup cider vinegar
1 tablespoon low-sodium soy sauce
2 cups cooked long-grain rice (cooked without
    salt or fat)
¼ cup slivered almonds, toasted

Peel and devein shrimp; set aside.

Combine peppers and onion in a 1-quart glass measure; cover with wax paper. Microwave at HIGH 2 to 3 minutes, stirring after every minute; set aside.

Drain pineapple, reserving ⅔ cup juice; set both aside. Combine brown sugar and next 3 ingredients in a 3-quart baking dish; stir well. Gradually add reserved ⅔ cup pineapple juice, vinegar, and soy sauce, stirring with a wire whisk until blended. Microwave at HIGH 6 to 7 minutes or until thickened and bubbly, stirring every 2 minutes.

Add shrimp, pepper mixture, and pineapple; cover dish with lid. Microwave at HIGH 6 to 7 minutes or until shrimp turn pink, stirring after 3 minutes. Let stand, uncovered, 3 minutes. Place rice on a large serving platter. Spoon shrimp mixture over rice and top with toasted almonds. Yield: 4 servings.

Note: To toast almonds in the microwave, spread slivered almonds in the bottom of a 1-quart baking dish coated with cooking spray. Microwave at HIGH 6 to 7 minutes, stirring every 30 seconds.

PER SERVING: 405 CALORIES (11% FROM FAT)
FAT 4.9G (SATURATED FAT 0.6G)
PROTEIN 21.5G CARBOHYDRATE 68.5G
CHOLESTEROL 129MG SODIUM 550MG

Polynesian Shrimp

SHRIMP CREOLE

2 pounds unpeeled medium-size fresh shrimp
Vegetable cooking spray
½ cup chopped green pepper
½ cup chopped onion
½ cup chopped celery
2 cloves garlic, minced
2 (14½-ounce) cans no-salt-added whole
    tomatoes, undrained and chopped
1 (8-ounce) can no-salt-added tomato sauce
1 tablespoon low-sodium Worcestershire sauce
1 teaspoon sugar
½ teaspoon salt
½ teaspoon chili powder
½ teaspoon hot sauce
2 teaspoons cornstarch
1 tablespoon water
3 cups cooked long-grain rice (cooked without
    salt or fat)

Peel and devein shrimp; set aside.

Coat a Dutch oven with cooking spray; place over medium-high heat until hot. Add green pepper, onion, celery, and garlic; sauté 5 minutes or until vegetables are tender. Add tomatoes and next 6 ingredients, stirring well. Cook, uncovered, over medium heat 15 minutes, stirring occasionally. Cover, reduce heat, and simmer 45 minutes.

Combine cornstarch and water in a small bowl, blending well; add to tomato mixture, stirring constantly. Add shrimp to mixture; simmer 5 minutes or until shrimp are done.

To serve, place ½ cup cooked rice in each individual serving bowl; spoon ¾ cup shrimp mixture over each serving. Yield: 6 servings.

PER SERVING: 289 CALORIES (7% FROM FAT)
FAT 2.3G (SATURATED FAT 0.4G)
PROTEIN 26.9G CARBOHYDRATE 38.9G
CHOLESTEROL 172MG SODIUM 413MG

SHRIMP AND MUSSELS MEDLEY

(pictured on cover)

1½ pounds unpeeled medium-size fresh
    shrimp
1 pound fresh mussels
Vegetable cooking spray
1 teaspoon olive oil
¾ cup chopped onion
⅔ cup chopped green pepper
⅔ cup chopped sweet red pepper
⅔ cup chopped sweet yellow pepper
5 cloves garlic, minced
2 cups peeled, seeded, and chopped tomato
1½ cups dry white wine
⅓ cup chopped fresh cilantro
¼ teaspoon salt
8 cups cooked linguine (cooked without salt
    or fat)

Peel and devein shrimp, leaving tails intact. Set aside. Remove beards on mussels, and scrub shells with a brush. Discard opened, cracked, or heavy mussels (they're filled with sand). Set aside.

Coat a Dutch oven with cooking spray; add oil. Place over medium-high heat until hot. Add onion and next 4 ingredients; sauté 3 minutes or until vegetables are tender. Add tomato, wine, cilantro, and salt; bring to a boil. Add shrimp and mussels. Cover and cook 8 minutes or until mussels are open and shrimp turn pink.

Place 1 cup cooked linguine in each individual serving bowl; spoon shrimp mixture evenly over linguine. Yield: 8 servings.

PER SERVING: 312 CALORIES (10% FROM FAT)
FAT 3.4G (SATURATED FAT 0.5G)
PROTEIN 22.4G CARBOHYDRATE 47.2G
CHOLESTEROL 101MG SODIUM 220MG

SHRIMP SCAMPI

2 pounds unpeeled large fresh shrimp
3 tablespoons margarine
1 cup chopped sweet red pepper
8 cloves garlic, crushed
½ cup dry white wine
¼ cup minced fresh parsley
¼ cup fresh lemon juice
½ teaspoon salt
¼ teaspoon pepper
Paprika
6 cups cooked angel hair pasta (cooked
    without salt or fat)
Lemon slices (optional)

Peel shrimp, leaving tails intact; devein. Starting at tail end, butterfly underside of each shrimp, cutting to, but not through, back of shrimp. Divide shrimp among 6 gratin dishes, arranging shrimp with cut sides up; set aside.

Melt margarine in a small skillet over medium heat. Add red pepper and garlic; sauté 2 minutes. Remove from heat; stir in wine and next 4 ingredients. Spoon wine mixture evenly over each serving; sprinkle paprika over shrimp. Place gratin dishes on a broiler pan, and broil 5½ inches from heat (with electric oven door partially opened) 6 minutes or until shrimp turn pink. Serve with pasta; garnish with lemon slices, if desired. Yield: 6 servings.

PER SERVING: 383 CALORIES (20% FROM FAT)
FAT 8.7G (SATURATED FAT 1.6G)
PROTEIN 29.9G CARBOHYDRATE 41.8G
CHOLESTEROL 172MG SODIUM 435MG

Shrimp Scampi

Fragrant Shrimp Brochettes (recipe on page 123)

OUTDOOR SPECIALTIES

*G*rilling fish and shellfish is the cooking method preferred by many chefs who specialize in seafood entrées. Grilling not only captures the real taste of seafood but also is a low-fat way to cook. Best of all, grilling is easy and mess-free.

Firm-textured fish, such as amberjack, mahimahi, and salmon, are perfect for grilling because the flesh holds together during cooking. Catfish, snapper, and other more tender fish can also be grilled, although a grilling basket is recommended.

Scallops and shrimp are ideal for skewering and grilling. Turn to page 122 for the first of several recipes. If you can't decide which to try first, start with Grilled Shrimp and Scallops (page 123)—it's simple, easy, and loaded with flavor.

HICKORY-GRILLED AMBERJACK WITH GRILLED SALSA

(pictured on page 2)

¼ cup balsamic vinegar
3 tablespoons water
1 teaspoon low-sodium Worcestershire sauce
½ teaspoon chicken-flavored bouillon granules
1 clove garlic, minced
6 (4-ounce) amberjack steaks (¾ inch thick)
Hickory chips
2 ears fresh corn in husks
1½ teaspoons reduced-calorie margarine, melted
1 teaspoon salt-free lemon-pepper seasoning
Vegetable cooking spray
2 small tomatoes
¼ cup chopped onion
1 tablespoon chopped fresh parsley
1 tablespoon balsamic vinegar
1 teaspoon olive oil
½ teaspoon sugar
¼ teaspoon salt
⅛ teaspoon freshly ground pepper
1 clove garlic, minced
Fresh parsley sprigs (optional)

Combine first 5 ingredients in a large heavy-duty, zip-top plastic bag. Add steaks. Seal bag, and shake until well coated. Chill 30 minutes.

Soak hickory chips in water 30 minutes.

Carefully peel back husks from corn, leaving husks attached. Remove and discard silks. Brush corn with margarine, and sprinkle evenly with lemon-pepper seasoning. Return husks to original position, and tie tips with wire twist-ties.

Place hickory chips on medium-hot coals (350° to 400°). Coat grill rack with cooking spray; place on grill over coals. Place corn on rack; grill, covered, 30 minutes or until tender, turning every 5 minutes. Place tomatoes on rack; grill, covered, 5 minutes or until skins split and separate from tomatoes.

Remove steaks from marinade; discard marinade. Place steaks on rack over medium-hot coals; grill, covered, 4 minutes on each side or until fish flakes easily when tested with a fork. Set aside; keep warm.

Remove husks from corn, and cut corn from cob. Peel tomatoes; seed and chop. Combine corn, tomato, onion, and next 7 ingredients in a medium bowl, stirring well. Transfer steaks to individual serving plates, and top evenly with salsa. Garnish with parsley sprigs, if desired. Yield: 6 servings.

PER SERVING: 159 CALORIES (19% FROM FAT)
FAT 3.3G (SATURATED FAT 0.5G)
PROTEIN 22.0G CARBOHYDRATE 10.6G
CHOLESTEROL 58MG SODIUM 225MG

CREOLE CATFISH FILLETS

2 tablespoons minced fresh onion
½ teaspoon dried thyme
¼ teaspoon grated lemon rind
⅛ teaspoon ground red pepper
3 tablespoons plain low-fat yogurt
1½ tablespoons nonfat mayonnaise
1½ tablespoons Creole or Dijon mustard
1 tablespoon reduced-calorie ketchup
1 teaspoon paprika
½ teaspoon onion powder
⅛ teaspoon salt
⅛ teaspoon ground red pepper
4 (4-ounce) farm-raised catfish fillets
Vegetable cooking spray
4 lemon wedges

Combine first 8 ingredients in a small bowl; stir well. Cover and chill.

Combine paprika and next 3 ingredients; stir well. Rub mixture over both sides of fillets. Arrange fillets in a wire grilling basket coated with cooking spray; place on grill rack over hot coals (400° to 500°). Grill, uncovered, 6 minutes on each side or until fish flakes easily when tested with a fork. Serve each fillet with a lemon wedge and 2 tablespoons sauce. Yield: 4 servings.

PER SERVING: 178 CALORIES (30% FROM FAT)
FAT 6.0G (SATURATED FAT 1.3G)
PROTEIN 22.7G CARBOHYDRATE 14.8G
CHOLESTEROL 66MG SODIUM 372MG

Zesty Catfish Spears

ZESTY CATFISH SPEARS

2 teaspoons grated lemon rind
½ teaspoon fennel seeds, crushed
¼ teaspoon salt
⅛ teaspoon pepper
2 (4-ounce) farm-raised catfish fillets
Vegetable cooking spray

   Combine first 4 ingredients; rub mixture on both sides of fillets. Cover and chill at least 4 hours.
   Cut each fillet lengthwise into 2 strips. Thread fillets evenly onto 4 (8-inch) skewers.
   Coat grill rack with cooking spray, and place on grill over medium-hot coals (350° to 400°). Place fish on rack, and grill, uncovered, 6 minutes on each side or until fish flakes easily when tested with a fork. Yield: 2 servings.

PER SERVING: 137 CALORIES (34% FROM FAT)
FAT 5.2G (SATURATED FAT 1.1G)
PROTEIN 20.7G CARBOHYDRATE 0.7G
CHOLESTEROL 66MG SODIUM 365MG

GRILLED GROUPER WITH AVOCADO AÏOLI

¼ cup low-sodium soy sauce
1 teaspoon grated lemon rind
¼ cup fresh lemon juice
2 tablespoons water
¼ teaspoon chicken-flavored bouillon granules
2 cloves garlic, crushed
8 (4-ounce) grouper fillets
Vegetable cooking spray
Avocado Aïoli
24 (¼-inch-thick) slices avocado (about 2
     medium)
8 (⅛-inch-thick) slices lemon, quartered
Fresh cilantro sprigs (optional)

Combine soy sauce, lemon rind, lemon juice, water, bouillon granules, and garlic in a large shallow dish. Place fillets in a single layer in dish, turning to coat. Cover and marinate in refrigerator 30 minutes, turning fillets once.

Remove fillets from marinade, reserving marinade. Bring marinade to a boil in a small saucepan; set aside. Coat grill rack with cooking spray; place rack on grill over medium-hot coals (350° to 400°). Place fillets on rack; grill, covered, 4 to 5 minutes on each side or until fish flakes easily when tested with a fork, basting fillets frequently with reserved marinade.

Transfer fillets to a serving platter, and top each fillet with 1 tablespoon Avocado Aïoli. Arrange avocado slices and lemon quarters evenly alongside fillets. Garnish with fresh cilantro sprigs, if desired. Yield: 8 servings.

Grilled Grouper with Avocado Aïoli

Avocado Aïoli

¼ cup mashed ripe avocado (about 1 small)
1 tablespoon minced fresh cilantro
3 tablespoons nonfat mayonnaise
2 tablespoons lime juice
1 clove garlic, crushed

Combine all ingredients in container of an electric blender; cover and process until smooth, stopping once to scrape down sides. Yield: ½ cup.

PER SERVING: 162 CALORIES (33% FROM FAT)
FAT 5.9G (SATURATED FAT 1.0G)
PROTEIN 22.6G CARBOHYDRATE 4.2G
CHOLESTEROL 41MG SODIUM 193MG

FLOUNDER GRILLED IN FOIL

Vegetable cooking spray
1 teaspoon margarine
½ cup (2-inch) julienne-sliced leeks
½ cup (2-inch) julienne-sliced carrot
1 tablespoon lemon juice
2 teaspoons chopped fresh tarragon
4 (4-ounce) flounder fillets
¼ teaspoon salt
⅛ teaspoon pepper

Coat a nonstick skillet with cooking spray; add margarine, and place over medium heat until margarine melts. Add leeks and carrot; sauté 3 minutes or until crisp-tender. Remove from heat; stir in lemon juice and tarragon, and set aside.

Fold 2 (16- x 12-inch) sheets of heavy-duty aluminum foil in half lengthwise. Open foil, and coat inside with cooking spray. Place 2 fillets on half of each foil sheet; sprinkle evenly with salt and pepper, and top with vegetable mixture. Fold foil over fillets; tightly seal edges. Place packets on grill rack over hot coals (400° to 500°), and grill, uncovered, 7 minutes. Yield: 4 servings.

PER SERVING: 133 CALORIES (18% FROM FAT)
FAT 2.6G (SATURATED FAT 0.5G)
PROTEIN 22.0G CARBOHYDRATE 4.4G
CHOLESTEROL 60MG SODIUM 259MG

HALIBUT WITH DRIED PINEAPPLE SALSA

You may substitute grouper, snapper, or large-flaked cod if halibut is not available.

½ cup diced dried pineapple
½ cup diced sweet red pepper
¼ cup chopped fresh cilantro
¼ cup fresh lime juice
2 teaspoons minced jalapeño pepper
1 teaspoon vegetable oil
⅛ teaspoon salt
4 (4-ounce) halibut steaks (about 1 inch thick)
1 teaspoon vegetable oil
⅛ teaspoon salt
Vegetable cooking spray
Lime wedges (optional)

Combine pineapple, sweet red pepper, cilantro, lime juice, jalapeño pepper, oil, and ⅛ teaspoon salt in a bowl, and stir well. Let pineapple salsa stand at least 15 minutes, stirring occasionally.

Brush halibut steaks evenly with 1 teaspoon oil, and sprinkle with ⅛ teaspoon salt. Set aside.

Coat grill rack with cooking spray; place on grill over medium-hot coals (350° to 400°). Place steaks on rack; grill, uncovered, 5 minutes on each side or until fish flakes easily with a fork. Serve each steak with ¼ cup pineapple salsa and lime wedges, if desired. Yield: 4 servings.

PER SERVING: 201 CALORIES (24% FROM FAT)
FAT 5.4G (SATURATED FAT 0.8G)
PROTEIN 24.6G CARBOHYDRATE 13.8G
CHOLESTEROL 53MG SODIUM 224MG

Grilled Mahimahi with Pineapple

GRILLED MAHIMAHI WITH PINEAPPLE

1½ cups unsweetened pineapple juice
¼ cup plus 2 tablespoons low-sodium soy
    sauce
3 tablespoons brown sugar
3 tablespoons minced green onions
1 tablespoon dark sesame oil
2 teaspoons peeled, minced gingerroot
1½ teaspoons minced garlic
½ teaspoon dried crushed red pepper
4 (4-ounce) mahimahi fillets
8 (½-inch-thick) slices fresh pineapple
Vegetable cooking spray
Fresh spinach leaves (optional)
Green onion curls (optional)

Combine first 8 ingredients; stir well. Place fillets and pineapple in a baking dish. Pour half of pineapple juice mixture over fillets and pineapple. Cover and marinate in refrigerator 2 hours, turning fillets and pineapple occasionally. Divide remaining pineapple juice mixture in half; set aside.

Remove fillets and pineapple from marinade; discard marinade. Coat grill rack with cooking spray; place on grill over medium-hot coals (350° to 400°). Place fillets and pineapple on rack; grill, covered, 5 to 6 minutes on each side or until fish flakes easily when tested with a fork and pineapple is tender, basting frequently with half of reserved pineapple juice mixture.

Pour remaining half of reserved pineapple juice mixture through a wire-mesh strainer into a small saucepan, discarding solids. Bring to a boil over medium heat. Remove from heat; set aside, and keep warm.

Transfer fillets and pineapple to a serving platter. Drizzle with warm pineapple juice mixture. If desired, garnish with spinach leaves and green onion curls. Yield: 4 servings.

PER SERVING: 248 CALORIES (14% FROM FAT)
FAT 3.9G (SATURATED FAT 0.6G)
PROTEIN 21.1G   CARBOHYDRATE 32.1G
CHOLESTEROL 80MG   SODIUM 491MG

GINGER-LIME MAHIMAHI

2 (12-ounce) mahimahi fillets
¼ cup lime juice
1 tablespoon honey
1 clove garlic, minced
1 (⅛-inch-thick) slice peeled gingerroot
Vegetable cooking spray

Cut each fillet into 3 equal pieces; place fish in a shallow baking dish. Combine lime juice and next 3 ingredients in a small bowl, stirring well; pour over fish. Cover and marinate in refrigerator 1 hour.

Remove fish from marinade, reserving marinade. Remove and discard gingerroot. Bring marinade to a boil in a small saucepan; set aside. Coat grill rack with cooking spray; place on grill over medium-hot coals (350° to 400°). Place fish on rack, and grill, uncovered, 8 minutes on each side or until fish flakes easily when tested with a fork, basting frequently with marinade. Yield: 6 servings.

PER SERVING: 109 CALORIES (7% FROM FAT)
FAT 0.9G (SATURATED FAT 0.2G)
PROTEIN 20.3G   CARBOHYDRATE 4.1G
CHOLESTEROL 49MG   SODIUM 70MG

MUSTARD-GLAZED POLLOCK

2 tablespoons Dijon mustard
1 teaspoon olive oil
1 teaspoon minced fresh chives
4 (4-ounce) pollock or other lean white fish fillets
Vegetable cooking spray
Purple kale (optional)
Fresh chives (optional)

Combine mustard, olive oil, and minced chives in a small bowl, stirring well; brush mustard mixture evenly over both sides of fillets.

Arrange fillets in a wire grilling basket coated with cooking spray; place on grill rack over hot coals (400° to 500°). Grill 2 to 4 minutes on each side or until fish flakes easily when tested with a fork. If desired, garnish with purple kale and fresh chives. Yield: 4 servings.

PER SERVING: 125 CALORIES (21% FROM FAT)
FAT 2.9G (SATURATED FAT 0.3G)
PROTEIN 22.1G   CARBOHYDRATE 0.5G
CHOLESTEROL 81MG   SODIUM 320MG

Grilling Tips

• Choose fish steaks, pan-dressed fish, or fillets that are at least ¾ inch thick.

• Coat the grill rack with vegetable cooking spray before grilling to keep the lean, fragile fish from sticking.

• Use a fish basket when grilling very tender, delicate fish. Coat the part of the basket where the fish will touch with cooking spray.

• Baste fish often with a marinade or other sauce during cooking to keep it moist and tender, especially when cooking lean fish such as flounder and grouper.

• Watch fish closely when grilling to prevent overcooking. Fish is done when it flakes easily when pricked with a fork.

ORIENTAL GRILLED SALMON

1½ tablespoons brown sugar
3 tablespoons water
1 tablespoon low-sodium soy sauce
2 teaspoons peeled, minced gingerroot
2 teaspoons minced green onions
2 teaspoons lemon juice
½ teaspoon minced garlic
Dash of dried crushed red pepper
2 (4-ounce) salmon steaks (½ inch thick)
Vegetable cooking spray
2 tablespoons nonfat mayonnaise
1 tablespoon finely chopped fresh cilantro
½ teaspoon peeled, grated gingerroot
¼ teaspoon crushed garlic
Fresh cilantro sprigs (optional)

Combine first 8 ingredients in a large heavy-duty, zip-top plastic bag; add salmon steaks. Seal bag, and marinate steaks in refrigerator 2 hours, turning bag occasionally. Remove salmon steaks from marinade, reserving marinade. Bring marinade to a boil in a small saucepan; set aside.

Coat grill rack with cooking spray; place on grill over medium-hot coals (350° to 400°). Place steaks on rack; grill, uncovered, 5 to 6 minutes on each side or until fish flakes easily when tested with a fork, basting frequently with reserved marinade.

Combine mayonnaise and next 3 ingredients, stirring well. Top each salmon steak with 1 tablespoon mayonnaise mixture. Garnish with fresh cilantro sprigs, if desired. Yield: 2 servings.

PER SERVING: 243 CALORIES (37% FROM FAT)
FAT 10.0G (SATURATED FAT 1.7G)
PROTEIN 24.5G   CARBOHYDRATE 11.9G
CHOLESTEROL 77MG   SODIUM 449MG

Oriental Grilled Salmon

Whole Salmon with Lemon-Rice Stuffing

2 teaspoons olive oil
1 cup finely chopped onion
1 cup sliced fresh mushrooms
1¾ cups long-grain rice, uncooked
½ teaspoon salt, divided
¼ teaspoon pepper
3 cups hot water
1 tablespoon grated lemon rind
2 teaspoons finely chopped fresh oregano
3 tablespoons fresh lemon juice
1 (4¾-pound) dressed salmon
Lemon slices (optional)
Fresh oregano sprigs (optional)

Heat olive oil in a large saucepan over medium heat until hot. Add onion and mushrooms; sauté 3 minutes. Add rice, ¼ teaspoon salt, and pepper; sauté 1 minute. Add hot water, lemon rind, and oregano; cover, reduce heat, and simmer 12 minutes or until liquid is absorbed. Remove from heat; add lemon juice, and toss. Set aside.

Place fish on a 25- x 18-inch sheet of heavy-duty aluminum foil; sprinkle inside of fish with remaining ¼ teaspoon salt. Stuff rice mixture into fish cavity; spoon remaining rice mixture onto foil. Wrap foil around rice mixture; pleat and crimp edges of foil to form a tray.

Place rack on grill prepared for indirect heat (see note below). Place foil-wrapped fish on unheated side of grill. Cover with grill lid, and cook 1 hour or until fish flakes easily when tested with a fork. (Do not turn fish.)

Remove fish and rice mixture from foil, and arrange on a serving platter. Remove skin from top side of fish; discard skin. If desired, garnish with lemon slices and oregano sprigs. Serve ¼ cup rice with each 3-ounce portion of cooked fish. Yield: 16 servings.

Note: For indirect heat, follow manufacturer's instructions for gas grills with dual controls, and ignite only one side of grill. Place fish on the other side of grill, close lid, and cook. When using a charcoal grill, bank charcoal to one side of grill, and ignite at 2-inch intervals. Once coals are coated with gray ash, place fish on grill on opposite side from charcoal. Cover with grill lid, and cook as directed in recipe.

Per Serving: 269 Calories (34% from Fat)
Fat 10.1g (Saturated Fat 1.8g)
Protein 24.9g   Carbohydrate 17.7g
Cholesterol 74mg   Sodium 131mg

Shark Steak Kabobs

2 pounds shark steaks (¾ inch thick)
3 tablespoons low-sodium soy sauce
2 tablespoons lemon juice
1 tablespoon dry sherry
2 teaspoons brown sugar
¼ teaspoon ground ginger
¼ teaspoon dry mustard
⅛ teaspoon garlic powder
2 small zucchini, cut into 8 (1-inch) slices
2 small yellow squash, cut into 8 (1-inch) slices
8 cherry tomatoes
8 medium-size fresh mushrooms
Vegetable cooking spray

Cut shark steaks into 1¼-inch pieces, and place in a shallow dish. Combine soy sauce and next 6 ingredients in a small bowl, stirring well; pour marinade over steak pieces. Cover and marinate in refrigerator 1 hour.

Remove steak pieces from marinade, reserving marinade. Bring marinade to a boil in a small saucepan; boil 2 minutes. Set aside.

Thread steak pieces, zucchini, yellow squash, tomatoes, and mushrooms alternately on 8 (12-inch) skewers. Coat grill rack with cooking spray; place on grill over medium-hot coals (350° to 400°). Place kabobs on rack, and grill, uncovered, 10 minutes or until fish flakes easily when tested with a fork, turning and basting occasionally with reserved marinade. Yield: 8 servings.

Per Serving: 140 Calories (28% from Fat)
Fat 4.3g (Saturated Fat 0.9g)
Protein 19.6g   Carbohydrate 4.2g
Cholesterol 45mg   Sodium 220mg

GRILLED RED SNAPPER WITH PESTO

1½ cups loosely packed fresh basil leaves
¼ cup tightly packed fresh parsley sprigs
¼ teaspoon salt
⅛ teaspoon pepper
1 small shallot, peeled and quartered
1 small clove garlic, peeled
1 tablespoon lemon juice
1 tablespoon olive oil
2 (8-ounce) red snapper fillets
Vegetable cooking spray
1 large tomato, cut into 8 wedges

Position knife blade in food processor bowl, and add basil leaves, parsley sprigs, salt, pepper, shallot, and garlic. Process until finely chopped. With processor running, slowly pour lemon juice and olive oil through food chute, blending until smooth.

Place fillets in a shallow dish. Spread 1 tablespoon basil mixture over both sides of fillets; cover and chill 30 minutes. Set aside the remaining basil mixture.

Arrange fillets in a wire grilling basket coated with cooking spray, and place on grill rack over medium-hot coals (350° to 400°). Grill, uncovered, 4 minutes on each side or until fish flakes easily when tested with a fork. Cut each fillet in half, and place on individual serving plates. Garnish each serving with 1 tablespoon basil mixture and 2 tomato wedges. Yield: 4 servings.

PER SERVING: 166 CALORIES (29% FROM FAT)
FAT 5.3G (SATURATED FAT 0.8G)
PROTEIN 24.2G CARBOHYDRATE 4.9G
CHOLESTEROL 42MG SODIUM 205MG

GRILLED ROSEMARY SWORDFISH

4 (4-ounce) swordfish steaks (about 1 inch thick)
1 teaspoon minced fresh rosemary
1 teaspoon grated lemon rind
1 clove garlic, minced
Vegetable cooking spray
1 tablespoon fresh lemon juice
¼ teaspoon pepper
Lemon wedges (optional)
Fresh rosemary sprigs (optional)

Arrange steaks in a large baking dish. Combine minced rosemary, lemon rind, and garlic; press evenly onto one side of each steak. Cover and chill 1 hour.

Coat grill rack with cooking spray; place rack on grill over medium-hot coals (350° to 400°). Place steaks on rack. Combine lemon juice and pepper, and brush over steaks. Grill, uncovered, 6 minutes on each side or until done, basting frequently with lemon juice mixture. Garnish with lemon wedges and rosemary sprigs, if desired. Yield: 4 servings.

PER SERVING: 136 CALORIES (30% FROM FAT)
FAT 4.6G (SATURATED FAT 1.2G)
PROTEIN 21.7G CARBOHYDRATE 0.8G
CHOLESTEROL 43MG SODIUM 98MG

Did You Know?

Swordfish is among the best choices of fish to grill. It has firm flesh and moderate to full flavor. Tuna and shark are suitable substitutes for swordfish.

Refer to the information on page 10 for other suggested fish and shellfish alternatives.

Grilled Rosemary Swordfish

Orange Julep Swordfish

ORANGE JULEP SWORDFISH

¼ cup unsweetened orange juice
3 tablespoons minced fresh mint
1 tablespoon peeled, grated gingerroot
1 tablespoon grated orange rind
2 tablespoons bourbon
2 (8-ounce) swordfish steaks (¾ inch thick)
4 (¼-inch-thick) slices orange
Vegetable cooking spray
Fresh mint sprigs (optional)

Combine first 5 ingredients in a large shallow dish. Place swordfish steaks and orange slices in a single layer in dish, turning to coat. Cover and marinate in refrigerator 30 minutes, turning once.

Coat grill rack with cooking spray; place on grill over medium-hot coals (350° to 400°). Remove steaks from marinade, discarding marinade. Place steaks on rack; grill, covered, 5 to 6 minutes on each side or until fish flakes easily when tested with a fork. Transfer steaks to a serving platter, and cut each steak in half.

Place orange slices on grill rack; grill, covered, 2 minutes on each side. Cut each slice into thirds, and arrange on serving platter. Garnish with fresh mint sprigs, if desired. Yield: 4 servings.

PER SERVING: 169 CALORIES (25% FROM FAT)
FAT 4.7G (SATURATED FAT 1.3G)
PROTEIN 23.1G   CARBOHYDRATE 7.9G
CHOLESTEROL 44MG   SODIUM 102MG

SWORDFISH KABOBS WITH RED PEPPER PESTO

2 tablespoons dry white wine
2½ teaspoons minced garlic, divided
1 teaspoon dried oregano
1 (8-ounce) swordfish steak
1 large sweet red pepper
2 tablespoons chopped fresh basil
1 teaspoon balsamic vinegar
½ teaspoon olive oil
⅛ teaspoon salt
Vegetable cooking spray

Combine wine, 2 teaspoons garlic, and oregano in a small bowl, stirring well. Cut swordfish steak into 1¼-inch cubes; add to wine mixture. Cover and marinate in refrigerator 1 hour.

Cut pepper in half lengthwise; remove and discard seeds and membrane. Place pepper, skin side up, on a baking sheet; flatten with palm of hand. Broil 5½ inches from heat (with electric oven door partially opened) 15 to 20 minutes or until charred. Place pepper in ice water until cool. Remove from water; peel and discard skin.

Position knife blade in food processor bowl; add roasted red pepper, remaining ½ teaspoon garlic, basil, and next 3 ingredients. Process until smooth. Transfer mixture to a small saucepan. Cook over medium heat until thoroughly heated. Remove from heat; set aside, and keep warm.

Remove swordfish from marinade, reserving marinade. Bring marinade to a boil in a small saucepan; set aside.

Thread fish onto 2 (10-inch) skewers. Coat grill rack with cooking spray; place on grill over medium-hot coals (350° to 400°). Place kabobs on rack; grill, uncovered, 4 to 5 minutes on each side or until fish flakes easily when tested with a fork, basting frequently with marinade. Serve kabobs with red pepper mixture. Yield: 2 servings.

PER SERVING: 177 CALORIES (33% FROM FAT)
FAT 6.4G (SATURATED FAT 1.5G)
PROTEIN 23.5G   CARBOHYDRATE 5.6G
CHOLESTEROL 44MG   SODIUM 253MG

HICKORY-SMOKED TROUT

Soaking the hickory chips in water before placing them on the grill keeps the chips from burning too quickly.

Hickory chips
8 (4-ounce) trout fillets
1½ cups water
½ cup firmly packed dark brown sugar
⅓ cup lemon juice
¼ teaspoon ground red pepper
Vegetable cooking spray
¼ teaspoon salt

Soak hickory chips in water for 30 minutes.

Place fillets in a large heavy-duty, zip-top plastic bag. Combine water and next 3 ingredients, stirring well. Pour over fillets; seal bag, and shake gently until fillets are well coated. Marinate in refrigerator 2 hours, turning bag occasionally.

Remove fillets from marinade, reserving marinade; set fillets and marinade aside.

Prepare charcoal fire in smoker; let burn 20 minutes. Place chips on coals. Place water pan in smoker; add hot water and reserved marinade to fill line on pan. Place fillets, skin side down, on smoker rack coated with cooking spray; sprinkle with salt. Cover with lid; cook 1 hour or until fish flakes easily when tested with a fork. Yield: 8 servings.

PER SERVING: 189 CALORIES (19% FROM FAT)
FAT 3.9G (SATURATED FAT 0.7G)
PROTEIN 23.4G   CARBOHYDRATE 14.2G
CHOLESTEROL 65MG   SODIUM 108MG

Cooking Tip

Good cooks often use marinades to enhance the flavor of grilled fish and shellfish. Since seafood marinates for flavor's sake, not for tenderness, be careful not to overdo. Follow the recipe instructions, and only marinate for the recommended amount of time.

GRILLED TUNA WITH HERBED MAYONNAISE

¼ cup nonfat mayonnaise
¼ cup plain nonfat yogurt
1 teaspoon chopped fresh oregano
1 teaspoon chopped fresh tarragon
1 teaspoon lemon juice
¼ teaspoon salt
¼ teaspoon pepper
4 (6-ounce) tuna steaks (about 1 inch thick)
Vegetable cooking spray

Combine first 5 ingredients in a small bowl; stir well, and set aside. Sprinkle salt and pepper over tuna steaks; set aside.

Coat grill rack with cooking spray; place on grill over medium-hot coals (350° to 400°). Place steaks on grill rack coated with cooking spray; grill, uncovered, 3 minutes on each side or until fish flakes easily when tested with a fork. Serve each steak with 2 tablespoons mayonnaise mixture. Yield: 4 servings.

PER SERVING: 186 CALORIES (28% FROM FAT)
FAT 5.7G (SATURATED FAT 1.5G)
PROTEIN 27.4G   CARBOHYDRATE 4.6G
CHOLESTEROL 44MG   SODIUM 392MG

When grilling seafood, you may want to baste it with the liquid used for marinating. Follow one of these procedures to prevent contamination from bacteria:

• Before you add the fish or shellfish, pour a portion of the marinade into a small bowl to save for basting. Before grilling, discard the marinade that was in contact with the raw fish.

or

• After marinating the fish or shellfish, drain the marinade into a saucepan, and bring it to a boil to destroy any bacteria from the uncooked fish.

SWEET-AND-SOUR TUNA STEAKS

¼ cup plus 2 tablespoons honey
¼ cup plus 2 tablespoons sherry vinegar
¼ cup low-sodium soy sauce
2 teaspoons peeled, minced gingerroot
4 cloves garlic, crushed
4 (4-ounce) yellowfin tuna steaks
Vegetable cooking spray
¼ teaspoon salt
⅛ teaspoon freshly ground pepper

Combine first 5 ingredients; pour half of mixture into a shallow dish, reserving remaining mixture.

Place tuna steaks in mixture in dish, turning to coat both sides of each steak. Cover and marinate in refrigerator 30 minutes, turning once. Remove steaks from marinade, discarding marinade.

Coat grill rack with cooking spray; place on grill over medium-hot coals (350° to 400°). Place steaks on rack; grill, uncovered, 5 minutes on one side. Turn; sprinkle with salt and pepper. Grill 4 to 5 minutes or until fish flakes easily when tested with a fork. To serve, spoon reserved honey mixture evenly over tuna steaks. Yield: 4 servings.

PER SERVING: 240 CALORIES (21% FROM FAT)
FAT 5.6G (SATURATED FAT 1.4G)
PROTEIN 26.7G   CARBOHYDRATE 16.7G
CHOLESTEROL 43MG   SODIUM 500MG

Cooktop Directions: Tuna may be prepared on the cooktop. Prepare honey mixture and marinate steaks as directed above. Heat 1½ teaspoons olive oil in a large nonstick skillet over medium-high heat. Add tuna steaks; cook 5 minutes on one side. Turn; sprinkle evenly with salt and pepper. Cook 5 to 6 minutes or until fish flakes easily when tested with a fork. Transfer tuna steaks to a serving platter; spoon reserved honey mixture evenly over tuna steaks. Yield: 4 servings.

PER SERVING: 256 CALORIES (26% FROM FAT)
FAT 7.3G (SATURATED FAT 1.7G)
PROTEIN 26.7G   CARBOHYDRATE 16.7G
CHOLESTEROL 43MG   SODIUM 500MG

Sweet-and-Sour Tuna Steak

GRILLED SCALLOPS WITH BLACK BEANS

1 pound sea scallops
1 teaspoon olive oil
½ teaspoon ground cumin
¼ teaspoon ground red pepper
Vegetable cooking spray
1 cup diced onion
2 teaspoons minced garlic
½ cup minced sweet red pepper
2 cups canned black beans, rinsed and drained
½ teaspoon ground cumin
1 teaspoon balsamic vinegar

Place scallops in a shallow dish. Combine olive oil, ½ teaspoon cumin, and ground red pepper; drizzle over scallops, and toss gently. Cover; marinate in refrigerator 30 minutes, stirring occasionally.

Coat a large nonstick skillet with cooking spray; place over medium-high heat until hot. Add onion and garlic; sauté until tender. Add sweet red pepper, and sauté until tender. Stir in black beans and ½ teaspoon cumin; sauté 3 minutes or until thoroughly heated. Remove from heat; stir in vinegar, and keep warm.

Remove scallops from marinade, discarding marinade; thread scallops onto 4 (8-inch) skewers. Coat grill rack with cooking spray; place on grill over medium coals (300° to 350°). Place skewers on rack; grill, uncovered, 3 minutes on each side or until scallops are opaque. Spoon warm black bean mixture evenly onto individual serving plates. Arrange grilled scallops evenly over black bean mixture. Yield: 4 servings.

PER SERVING: 266 CALORIES (10% FROM FAT)
FAT 3.1G (SATURATED FAT 0.4G)
PROTEIN 28.7G   CARBOHYDRATE 31.4G
CHOLESTEROL 37MG   SODIUM 460MG

Grilled Scallops with Black Beans

GRILLED SHRIMP AND SCALLOPS

¼ pound unpeeled large fresh shrimp
¼ pound sea scallops
1 tablespoon minced shallots
2 tablespoons dry white wine
1 tablespoon lemon juice
2 teaspoons chopped fresh basil
2 teaspoons chopped fresh oregano
1 teaspoon minced garlic
2 teaspoons white wine Worcestershire sauce
1 teaspoon olive oil
⅛ teaspoon pepper
Vegetable cooking spray
2 teaspoons chopped fresh parsley
Lemon wedges (optional)

Peel and devein shrimp. Place shrimp and scallops in a heavy-duty, zip-top plastic bag. Combine shallots and next 8 ingredients; pour over shrimp and scallops. Seal bag, and shake until shrimp and scallops are well coated. Marinate in refrigerator 1 hour, turning bag occasionally.

Remove shrimp and scallops from marinade, reserving marinade. Bring marinade to a boil in a small saucepan; set aside. Thread shrimp and scallops onto 2 (12-inch) skewers.

Coat grill rack with cooking spray; place on grill over medium-hot coals (350° to 400°). Place kabobs on rack; grill, uncovered, 3 minutes on each side or until scallops are opaque, basting frequently with marinade. Place a kabob on each serving plate, and sprinkle with parsley. Garnish with lemon wedges, if desired. Yield: 2 servings.

PER SERVING: 122 CALORIES (26% FROM FAT)
FAT 3.5G (SATURATED FAT 0.5G)
PROTEIN 17.4G CARBOHYDRATE 4.7G
CHOLESTEROL 102MG SODIUM 224MG

FRAGRANT SHRIMP BROCHETTES

(pictured on page 106)

Use a citrus reamer or juicer to extract the intense, natural flavor of freshly squeezed citrus juice—the flavors of bottled juices don't compare.

1½ pounds unpeeled jumbo fresh shrimp
⅓ cup fresh grapefruit juice
¼ cup coarsely chopped fresh cilantro
¼ cup coarsely chopped fresh mint
¼ cup fresh orange juice
2 tablespoons fresh lime juice
¼ teaspoon salt
¼ teaspoon cracked pepper
Olive oil-flavored vegetable cooking spray
3 cups cooked rice (cooked without salt or fat)
Fresh cilantro sprigs (optional)

Peel and devein shrimp; leave tails intact. Combine grapefruit juice and next 6 ingredients in a large bowl. Add shrimp; toss well. Cover and marinate in refrigerator 30 minutes.

Remove shrimp from marinade, discarding marinade. Thread shrimp evenly onto 4 (10-inch) metal skewers. Coat shrimp with cooking spray.

Coat grill rack with cooking spray; place on grill over medium-hot coals (350° to 400°). Place skewers on rack; grill, covered, 3 minutes on each side or until shrimp turn pink. Serve over rice. Garnish with cilantro sprigs, if desired. Yield: 4 servings.

PER SERVING: 285 CALORIES (5% FROM FAT)
FAT 1.6G (SATURATED FAT 0.3G)
PROTEIN 26.9G CARBOHYDRATE 38.4G
CHOLESTEROL 221MG SODIUM 326MG

Southwestern Grilled Shrimp

SOUTHWESTERN GRILLED SHRIMP

1½ pounds unpeeled large fresh shrimp
2 tablespoons fresh lime juice, divided
1 tablespoon water
1 tablespoon low-sodium soy sauce
1 teaspoon minced garlic
1 teaspoon olive oil
1 jalapeño pepper, seeded and halved
3 tomatillos, husked
¼ cup plus 2 tablespoons cubed avocado
¼ teaspoon sugar
⅛ teaspoon salt
⅛ teaspoon freshly ground pepper
Vegetable cooking spray
Sweet red pepper strips (optional)
Fresh cilantro sprigs (optional)

Peel and devein shrimp; place in a large heavy-duty, zip-top plastic bag. Combine 1 tablespoon lime juice and next 4 ingredients; pour over shrimp. Seal bag, and shake gently. Marinate in refrigerator 2 hours.

Place pepper, skin side up, on a baking sheet; flatten with palm of hand. Broil 5½ inches from heat (with electric oven door partially opened) 10 minutes or until charred. Place in ice water until cool. Remove from water; peel and discard skin. Coarsely chop pepper; place in container of an electric blender. Coarsely chop tomatillos. Add tomatillos, remaining 1 tablespoon lime juice, avocado, and next 3 ingredients to blender container; cover and process until smooth. Chill.

Remove shrimp from marinade; discard marinade. Thread shrimp onto 4 (8-inch) skewers. Coat grill rack with cooking spray; place on grill over medium-hot coals (350° to 400°). Place shrimp on rack; grill, covered, 3 to 4 minutes on each side or until shrimp turn pink. Remove shrimp from skewers, and place on serving plates. Serve with tomatillo mixture. If desired, garnish with pepper strips and cilantro sprigs. Yield: 4 servings.

PER SERVING: 138 CALORIES (30% FROM FAT)
FAT 4.6G (SATURATED FAT 0.8G)
PROTEIN 19.9G CARBOHYDRATE 3.7G
CHOLESTEROL 180MG SODIUM 379MG

MIXED GRILL KABOBS

½ pound unpeeled medium-size fresh shrimp
½ pound amberjack fillets
1 (8-ounce) tuna steak (1 inch thick)
½ pound sea scallops
2 tablespoons white wine vinegar
2 tablespoons water
1 tablespoon vegetable oil
1 tablespoon plus 1 teaspoon honey
2 teaspoons prepared horseradish
2 teaspoons minced garlic
2 teaspoons dry mustard
2 teaspoons dried thyme
Vegetable cooking spray

Peel and devein shrimp, leaving tails intact. Cut amberjack and tuna into 8 pieces each. Place fish, shrimp, and scallops in a shallow dish. Combine vinegar and next 7 ingredients; pour over shrimp mixture. Cover and marinate in refrigerator 1 hour, stirring occasionally.

Remove shrimp mixture from marinade, discarding marinade. Alternate fish, shrimp, and scallops on 8 (10-inch) skewers. Coat grill rack with cooking spray, and place on grill over medium-hot coals (350° to 400°). Place kabobs on rack, and grill, uncovered, 4 to 5 minutes on each side or until fish flakes easily when tested with a fork and scallops are opaque. Yield: 8 servings.

PER SERVING: 137 CALORIES (29% FROM FAT)
FAT 4.4G (SATURATED FAT 1.0G)
PROTEIN 20.4G CARBOHYDRATE 2.8G
CHOLESTEROL 53MG SODIUM 83MG

Grilling Kabobs

• If you use bamboo skewers, soak them in water two hours before using to reduce charring and flammability.

• When you grill a large number of kabobs, place them in a wire basket—they'll be easier to turn.

Garlic Flounder (recipe on page 130)

QUICK & EASY MAIN DISHES

*I*f you need quick recipes, you've already discovered that this cookbook is for you! Not many entrées can be prepared as quickly as fish or shellfish. But to help you get in and out of the kitchen in record time, we collected some of the superfast recipes in one chapter.

In the following pages, you'll find recipes that call for 10 or fewer ingredients. You can prepare any of the dishes in 30 minutes or less (not including marinating or chilling time). And, like other recipes in this book, these are prepared the low-fat way—with limited amounts of butter and oil.

Even recipes like Crispy Pan-Fried Catfish (page 128) and Sautéed Soft-Shell Crabs (page 137) scale in under 30 percent fat. Try these, and you'll be guarding your health *and* your time.

BLACKENED AMBERJACK

1 (1-pound) amberjack fillet
1 tablespoon paprika
2 teaspoons onion powder
2 teaspoons garlic powder
1 teaspoon dried thyme
1 teaspoon dried oregano
1 teaspoon black pepper
½ teaspoon ground red pepper
Vegetable cooking spray

Cut fillet into 4 equal pieces. Combine paprika and next 6 ingredients in a small bowl; stir well. Dredge fish in spice mixture; let stand 5 minutes.

Coat a large cast-iron skillet with cooking spray; place over high heat until very hot. Add fish, and cook 3 minutes. Turn fish, and cook 3 to 4 additional minutes or until fish flakes easily when tested with a fork. Fish should look charred. (You may prefer to do this procedure outside due to the small amount of smoke that is created.) Yield: 4 servings.

PER SERVING: 182 CALORIES (30% FROM FAT)
FAT 6.0G (SATURATED FAT 1.5G)
PROTEIN 27.2G CARBOHYDRATE 3.8G
CHOLESTEROL 43MG SODIUM 46MG

BLUEFISH BAKE WITH LEMON AND ROSEMARY

Bluefish has soft, blue-gray flesh that lightens when cooked. Before cooking, remove the dark, fatty strip of flesh that runs through the center along the side of the fish.

4 (4-ounce) bluefish fillets
¼ cup fresh lemon juice
1 teaspoon dried rosemary, crushed
¼ teaspoon salt
⅛ teaspoon pepper
2 cloves garlic, minced

Place fillets in an 11- x 7- x 1½-inch baking dish. Pour lemon juice over fillets, and sprinkle with rosemary and remaining ingredients. Cover and marinate in refrigerator 1 hour, turning fillets occasionally.

Uncover and bake at 450° for 10 to 15 minutes or until fish flakes easily when tested with a fork. Yield: 4 servings.

Note: Substitute black sea bass, pompano, or sockeye salmon for bluefish, if desired. Cooking time may vary.

PER SERVING: 148 CALORIES (30% FROM FAT)
FAT 4.9G (SATURATED FAT 1.0G)
PROTEIN 22.9G CARBOHYDRATE 2.0G
CHOLESTEROL 67MG SODIUM 215MG

CRISPY PAN-FRIED CATFISH

1 egg white, lightly beaten
1 tablespoon water
¼ cup yellow cornmeal
2 tablespoons grated Parmesan cheese
1 tablespoon chopped fresh thyme
¼ teaspoon pepper
4 (4-ounce) farm-raised catfish fillets
3 tablespoons all-purpose flour
Vegetable cooking spray
Lemon wedges (optional)

Combine egg white and water; stir well, and set aside. Combine cornmeal and next 3 ingredients. Dredge fillets in flour; dip in egg white mixture, and dredge in cornmeal mixture.

Coat a large nonstick skillet with cooking spray, and place over medium-high heat until hot. Add fillets, and cook 3 minutes on each side or until fish flakes easily when tested with a fork. Transfer to a serving platter; garnish with lemon wedges, if desired. Yield: 4 servings.

PER SERVING: 202 CALORIES (27% FROM FAT)
FAT 6.0G (SATURATED FAT 1.6G)
PROTEIN 23.9G CARBOHYDRATE 11.5G
CHOLESTEROL 68MG SODIUM 132MG

Vegetable-Topped Flounder

VEGETABLE-TOPPED FLOUNDER

8 (4-ounce) flounder fillets
Vegetable cooking spray
1 teaspoon lemon juice
¼ teaspoon pepper
¼ cup frozen apple juice concentrate, thawed
½ cup diced onion
½ cup diced celery
¼ cup diced green pepper
¼ cup diced sweet red pepper
2 teaspoons sesame seeds, toasted

Place fillets in a 13- x 9- x 2-inch baking dish coated with cooking spray. Drizzle with lemon juice, and sprinkle with pepper.

Combine apple juice concentrate and next 4 ingredients in a small nonstick skillet. Bring to a boil; reduce heat, and simmer until vegetables are crisp-tender. Spoon mixture evenly over fillets. Bake at 350° for 20 minutes or until fish flakes easily when tested with a fork.

Transfer fillets and vegetables to individual plates, using a slotted spoon; sprinkle with sesame seeds. Yield: 8 servings.

PER SERVING: 130 CALORIES (13% FROM FAT)
FAT 1.9G (SATURATED FAT 0.4G)
PROTEIN 21.9G   CARBOHYDRATE 5.4G
CHOLESTEROL 60MG   SODIUM 104MG

GARLIC FLOUNDER

(pictured on page 126)

6 (4-ounce) flounder fillets
¼ cup low-sodium soy sauce
2 tablespoons minced garlic
1½ tablespoons lemon juice
2 teaspoons sugar
1 tablespoon mixed peppercorns, crushed
Vegetable cooking spray
Fresh parsley sprigs (optional)

Place fillets in a shallow baking dish. Combine soy sauce and next 3 ingredients; pour over fillets. Cover and marinate in refrigerator 30 minutes.

Remove fillets from marinade; discard marinade. Sprinkle fillets evenly with peppercorns, pressing firmly so that pepper adheres to fillets.

Place fillets on rack of a broiler pan coated with cooking spray. Broil 5½ inches from heat (with electric oven door partially opened) 8 to 10 minutes or until fish flakes easily when tested with a fork. Transfer to a serving platter, and garnish with parsley sprigs, if desired. Yield: 6 servings.

PER SERVING: 114 CALORIES (12% FROM FAT)
FAT 1.5G (SATURATED FAT 0.3G)
PROTEIN 21.6G CARBOHYDRATE 2.0G
CHOLESTEROL 60MG SODIUM 223MG

GLAZED MAHIMAHI

3 tablespoons honey
3 tablespoons sherry vinegar
1 teaspoon peeled, minced gingerroot
4 cloves garlic, crushed
4 (4-ounce) mahimahi or other firm white fish
   fillets (about 1 inch thick)
1½ teaspoons olive oil
¼ teaspoon salt
⅛ teaspoon freshly ground pepper

Combine first 4 ingredients in a shallow dish; stir well. Add fillets, turning to coat. Cover and marinate in refrigerator 20 minutes. Remove fillets from marinade, reserving marinade.

Heat olive oil in a large nonstick skillet over medium-high heat. Add fillets; cook 6 minutes. Turn fillets; sprinkle with salt and pepper. Cook 6 minutes or until fish flakes easily when tested with a fork. Remove from skillet; set aside.

Add reserved marinade to skillet; scrape bottom of skillet with a spoon to loosen browned particles. Bring to a boil, and cook 1 minute. To serve, spoon sauce over fillets. Yield: 4 servings.

PER SERVING: 184 CALORIES (14% FROM FAT)
FAT 2.9G (SATURATED FAT 0.5G)
PROTEIN 22.2G CARBOHYDRATE 14.7G
CHOLESTEROL 42MG SODIUM 274MG

LEMON-DILL FISH

4 (4-ounce) orange roughy or other lean
   white fish fillets
Vegetable cooking spray
¼ teaspoon salt
½ cup Lemon-Dill Coating
Lemon wedges (optional)

Coat both sides of fillets with cooking spray; sprinkle with salt. Place ½ cup Lemon-Dill Coating in a dish; dredge fillets in topping. Place in an 11- x 7- x 1½-inch baking dish coated with cooking spray. Bake at 400° for 15 minutes or until fish flakes easily when tested with a fork. Serve with lemon wedges, if desired. Yield: 4 servings.

LEMON-DILL COATING
2 cups finely crushed plain Melba toast rounds
2 tablespoons paprika
2 tablespoons grated lemon rind
1 tablespoon plus 1 teaspoon dried dillweed
1½ teaspoons dry mustard

Combine all ingredients in large heavy-duty, zip-top plastic bag; seal and shake well. Store in refrigerator; shake well before each use. Use as a coating mix for fish or chicken. Yield: 2 cups.

PER SERVING: 125 CALORIES (16% FROM FAT)
FAT 2.2G (SATURATED FAT 0.2G)
PROTEIN 18.3G CARBOHYDRATE 7.6G
CHOLESTEROL 23MG SODIUM 307MG

Lemon-Dill Fish

Steamed Orange Roughy with Herbs

STEAMED ORANGE ROUGHY WITH HERBS

This unbelievably simple recipe has so much flavor that you won't need to reach for the salt shaker.

½ cup fresh parsley sprigs
½ cup fresh chives
½ cup fresh thyme sprigs
½ cup fresh rosemary sprigs
2 (8-ounce) orange roughy fillets
Lemon slices

Arrange half of herbs in bottom of a steamer basket. Top with fillets and remaining herbs.

Cover and steam fillets 7 minutes or until fish flakes easily when tested with a fork. Serve with lemon slices. Yield: 4 servings.

Note: Any mild-flavored fish can be substituted in this recipe. Try cod, grouper, or snapper.

PER SERVING: 79 CALORIES (10% FROM FAT)
FAT 0.8G (SATURATED FAT 0.0G)
PROTEIN 16.7G CARBOHYDRATE 0.0G
CHOLESTEROL 23MG SODIUM 72MG

ORANGE-BAKED SNAPPER

4 (4-ounce) red snapper fillets (about ¾ inch thick)
Vegetable cooking spray
1¼ cups unsweetened orange juice, divided
¼ teaspoon ground cloves, divided
2 teaspoons cornstarch
2 medium oranges, peeled, sectioned, and seeded (about 1 cup)

Arrange fillets in a 10- x 6- x 2-inch baking dish coated with cooking spray.

Combine ½ cup orange juice and ⅛ teaspoon cloves; stir well. Pour orange juice mixture over fillets; cover and chill at least 30 minutes.

Bake, uncovered, at 400° for 20 minutes or until fish flakes easily when tested with a fork, basting occasionally with orange juice mixture. Transfer fillets to a serving platter, and keep warm.

Combine remaining ¾ cup orange juice and cornstarch in a small nonaluminum saucepan, stirring with a wire whisk until blended. Bring to a boil; cook, stirring constantly, 1 minute or until mixture is thickened. Remove from heat; stir in remaining ⅛ teaspoon cloves and orange sections. To serve, spoon sauce over fish. Yield: 4 servings.

PER SERVING: 174 CALORIES (9% FROM FAT)
FAT 1.8G (SATURATED FAT 0.3G)
PROTEIN 24.2G CARBOHYDRATE 14.5G
CHOLESTEROL 42MG SODIUM 74MG

ORIENTAL RED SNAPPER

½ cup thinly sliced green onions
1 to 1½ tablespoons peeled, minced gingerroot
2 tablespoons low-sodium soy sauce
2 tablespoons unsweetened pineapple juice
1 teaspoon sugar
1 teaspoon dark sesame oil
¼ teaspoon salt
¼ to ½ teaspoon dried crushed red pepper
2 cloves garlic, crushed
4 (4-ounce) red snapper fillets

Combine first 9 ingredients; stir well. Place fillets in a shallow dish; spread green onion mixture evenly over fillets. Cover and marinate in refrigerator 30 minutes.

Line a steamer basket with a heat-resistant plate at least 1 inch smaller in diameter than the basket. Transfer fillets to plate, using a slotted spoon; discard marinade. Place steamer basket over boiling water. Cover; steam 10 minutes or until fish flakes easily when tested with a fork. Yield: 4 servings.

PER SERVING: 143 CALORIES (17% FROM FAT)
FAT 2.7G (SATURATED FAT 0.5G)
PROTEIN 23.7G CARBOHYDRATE 4.1G
CHOLESTEROL 42MG SODIUM 395MG

CURRY-SPICED SWORDFISH STEAKS

For a quick meal, serve these fish steaks with couscous and steamed snow peas.

½ teaspoon curry powder
¼ teaspoon salt
¼ teaspoon ground cumin
⅛ teaspoon ground turmeric
1 large clove garlic, minced
Dash of ground red pepper
4 (4-ounce) swordfish steaks
2 tablespoons plain nonfat yogurt
1 tablespoon chopped fresh cilantro

Combine first 6 ingredients; stir well. Rub mixture over both sides of swordfish steaks. Place steaks in a 9-inch square baking dish. Cover with heavy-duty plastic wrap, and vent. Microwave at HIGH 6 to 7 minutes, rotating dish a quarter-turn after 3 minutes.

Remove steaks from dish; set aside, and keep warm. Strain cooking liquid from dish into a 1-cup glass measure; microwave cooking liquid, uncovered, at HIGH 30 seconds. Stir in yogurt and chopped cilantro. Spoon sauce over swordfish. Yield: 4 servings.

PER SERVING: 144 CALORIES (29% FROM FAT)
FAT 4.6G (SATURATED FAT 1.3G)
PROTEIN 23.0G CARBOHYDRATE 1.1G
CHOLESTEROL 44MG SODIUM 255MG

Curry-Spiced Swordfish Steak

BROILED RAINBOW TROUT

2 (10-ounce) whole rainbow trout, dressed
½ cup canned low-sodium chicken broth, undiluted
2 teaspoons minced garlic
2 teaspoons dried basil
2 teaspoons dried oregano
2 teaspoons balsamic vinegar
½ teaspoon sesame oil
Vegetable cooking spray
6 thin slices lemon
Lemon wedges (optional)

Place trout in a large heavy-duty, zip-top plastic bag. Combine chicken broth, minced garlic, basil, oregano, vinegar, and oil; pour over fish. Seal bag, and marinate in refrigerator 3 hours, turning bag occasionally.

Remove fish from marinade, and discard marinade. Place fish on rack of a broiler pan coated with cooking spray. Place 3 lemon slices in each fish cavity. Broil 5½ inches from heat (with electric oven door partially opened) 4 minutes on each side or until fish flakes easily when tested with a fork. Garnish with lemon wedges, if desired. Yield: 2 servings.

PER SERVING: 115 CALORIES (29% FROM FAT)
FAT 3.7G (SATURATED FAT 0.6G)
PROTEIN 18.6G   CARBOHYDRATE 0.8G
CHOLESTEROL 51MG   SODIUM 29MG

PEPPERCORN TUNA

2 (4-ounce) tuna steaks (¾ inch thick)
½ teaspoon olive oil
¼ teaspoon salt
1 teaspoon whole black peppercorns, crushed
½ teaspoon whole pink peppercorns, crushed
½ teaspoon whole green peppercorns, crushed
Lemon wedges (optional)
Fresh sage sprigs (optional)

Brush both sides of each tuna steak evenly with oil; sprinkle with salt. Combine crushed peppercorns; press into both sides of each steak.

Place a medium cast-iron skillet over high heat until almost smoking. Add steaks; cook 4 to 5 minutes on each side or until fish flakes easily when tested with a fork. Transfer to a serving platter. If desired, garnish with lemon wedges and sage sprigs. Yield: 2 servings.

PER SERVING: 179 CALORIES (34% FROM FAT)
FAT 6.8G (SATURATED FAT 1.6G)
PROTEIN 26.7G   CARBOHYDRATE 1.4G
CHOLESTEROL 43MG   SODIUM 338MG

STEAMED CLAMS

3 dozen cherrystone clams
2 tablespoons cornmeal
¾ cup water
⅓ cup dry white wine
1½ tablespoons Old Bay seasoning
½ teaspoon ground white pepper
Lemon wedges (optional)

Scrub clams thoroughly with a brush, discarding any that are cracked or open. Place remaining clams in a large bowl; cover with cold water, and sprinkle with cornmeal. Let stand 30 minutes. Drain and rinse clams, discarding cornmeal. Set clams aside.

Combine ¾ cup water and next 3 ingredients in a large Dutch oven; bring mixture to a boil. Add clams; cover, reduce heat, and simmer 10 to 12 minutes or until clams open. Remove and discard any unopened clams.

Remove remaining clams with a slotted spoon, reserving liquid, if desired. Serve clams immediately with reserved liquid and lemon wedges, if desired. Yield: 4 servings.

PER SERVING: 128 CALORIES (12% FROM FAT)
FAT 1.7G (SATURATED FAT 0.2G)
PROTEIN 21.8G   CARBOHYDRATE 4.8G
CHOLESTEROL 58MG   SODIUM 204MG

Angel Hair Pasta with Fresh Clams

ANGEL HAIR PASTA WITH FRESH CLAMS

12 littleneck clams
2 teaspoons cornmeal
Olive oil-flavored vegetable cooking spray
1½ teaspoons minced garlic
2 cups peeled, seeded, and chopped tomato
¼ cup clam juice
¼ cup dry white wine
⅛ teaspoon dried crushed red pepper
4 ounces capellini (angel hair pasta), uncooked
1½ teaspoons chopped flat-leaf parsley

Scrub clams thoroughly with a brush, discarding any that are cracked or open. Place remaining clams in a large bowl; cover with cold water, and sprinkle with cornmeal. Let stand 30 minutes. Drain and rinse clams, discarding cornmeal. Set clams aside.

Coat a medium nonstick skillet with cooking spray. Place over medium-high heat until hot. Add garlic, and sauté 30 seconds. Add tomato and next 3 ingredients. Bring to a boil; reduce heat, and simmer, uncovered, 15 minutes, stirring occasionally.

Place clams on top of tomato mixture. Cover and cook 8 minutes or until clams open. Remove and discard any unopened clams.

Cook pasta according to package directions, omitting salt and fat. Drain. Remove clams from tomato mixture; set aside. Toss pasta with tomato mixture, and transfer to serving plates. Arrange clams evenly over pasta. Sprinkle with parsley. Yield: 2 servings.

PER SERVING: 282 CALORIES (7% FROM FAT)
FAT 2.2G (SATURATED FAT 0.3G)
PROTEIN 12.9G   CARBOHYDRATE 53.4G
CHOLESTEROL 9MG   SODIUM 106MG

CLAM LINGUINE

8 ounces linguine, uncooked
Vegetable cooking spray
1 tablespoon olive oil
4 large cloves garlic, minced
3 (6½-ounce) cans minced clams, undrained
¼ cup grated Parmesan cheese, divided
Freshly ground pepper

Cook pasta according to package directions, omitting salt and fat. Drain pasta, and set aside.

Coat a large nonstick skillet with cooking spray; add olive oil, and place over medium-high heat until hot. Add garlic, and sauté 2 minutes.

Drain clams, reserving liquid. Add reserved clam liquid to pan, and cook 4 minutes. Add clams, and cook until thoroughly heated.

Add pasta, and toss well. Cook 2 minutes, stirring frequently.

Remove from heat. Add 3 tablespoons Parmesan cheese, tossing well. Spoon onto a serving platter. Sprinkle with remaining 1 tablespoon cheese, and serve with freshly ground pepper. Yield: 6 (1-cup) servings.

PER SERVING: 234 CALORIES (18% FROM FAT)
FAT 4.7G (SATURATED FAT 1.1G)
PROTEIN 15.7G CARBOHYDRATE 31.2G
CHOLESTEROL 26MG SODIUM 227MG

SAUTÉED SOFT-SHELL CRABS

4 soft-shell crabs, cleaned
2 tablespoons all-purpose flour
2 tablespoons yellow cornmeal
½ teaspoon ground red pepper
¼ cup skim milk
Vegetable cooking spray
1 teaspoon vegetable oil
2 tablespoons lemon juice
2 teaspoons chopped fresh parsley

Rinse crabs thoroughly with cold water. Pat dry with paper towels.

Combine flour, cornmeal, and pepper in a shallow dish. Dip crabs in milk, and dredge in flour mixture. Coat a large nonstick skillet with cooking spray; add oil. Place over medium-high heat until hot. Add crabs; cook 2 to 3 minutes on each side or until browned. Transfer to a serving plate. Sprinkle evenly with lemon juice and chopped parsley. Yield: 2 servings.

PER SERVING: 196 CALORIES (19% FROM FAT)
FAT 4.2G (SATURATED FAT 0.7G)
PROTEIN 23.6G CARBOHYDRATE 14.6G
CHOLESTEROL 94MG SODIUM 357MG

MUSSELS ANTIPASTO

Tightly shut shells mean that the mussels are fresh and still alive. Select small ones for the most tender mussels.

2 pounds fresh mussels
½ cup water
⅓ cup dry white wine
3 tablespoons diced carrot
3 tablespoons diced celery
2 tablespoons chopped fresh parsley
⅛ teaspoon dried crushed red pepper
1 clove garlic, sliced
1 bay leaf
2 tablespoons sliced green onions

Remove beards on mussels, and scrub shells with a brush. Discard opened, cracked, or heavy mussels (they're filled with sand). Set aside remaining mussels.

Combine water and next 7 ingredients in a large saucepan; bring to a boil. Reduce heat, and simmer 2 to 3 minutes. Add mussels; bring to a boil. Cover and cook 3 to 4 minutes or until shells open. Remove and discard bay leaf and any unopened mussels. Remove from heat; stir in green onions. Ladle mixture evenly into individual serving bowls. Yield: 4 servings.

PER SERVING: 118 CALORIES (20% FROM FAT)
FAT 2.6G (SATURATED FAT 0.5G)
PROTEIN 13.8G CARBOHYDRATE 6.0G
CHOLESTEROL 32MG SODIUM 220MG

CITRUS SCALLOPS WITH PEAS IN PARCHMENT

1 pound sea scallops
¼ cup sliced green onions
2 tablespoons frozen orange juice concentrate,
    thawed and undiluted
1 teaspoon peeled, grated gingerroot
¾ teaspoon curry powder
¼ teaspoon pepper
⅛ teaspoon salt
½ pound fresh Sugar Snap peas, trimmed

Combine first 7 ingredients in a medium bowl. Toss well, and set aside.

Cut 4 (15- x 14-inch) pieces of parchment paper; fold each in half crosswise, creasing firmly, and trim into a heart shape. Unfold hearts, and place on baking sheets.

Place ½ cup scallop mixture on each parchment heart, near the crease; arrange Sugar Snap peas around scallop mixture.

Fold over remaining half of each parchment heart. Starting with rounded edge, pleat and crimp edges of parchment together to make a seal; twist ends tightly to seal.

Bake at 400° for 10 minutes or until puffed and lightly browned. Place on individual serving plates, and cut open; serve immediately. Yield: 4 servings.

PER SERVING: 140 CALORIES (7% FROM FAT)
FAT 1.1G (SATURATED FAT 0.1G)
PROTEIN 20.9G CARBOHYDRATE 10.9G
CHOLESTEROL 37MG SODIUM 257MG

Citrus Scallops with Peas in Parchment

LEMON-SAUCED SCALLOPS

¾ cup all-purpose flour
¼ teaspoon ground white pepper
1½ pounds fresh bay scallops
3 egg whites, lightly beaten
Vegetable cooking spray
1 tablespoon plus 1 teaspoon reduced-calorie margarine, divided
⅔ cup dry white wine
½ cup sliced green onions
¼ cup lemon juice
⅛ teaspoon salt

Combine flour and white pepper in a small shallow dish, stirring well. Dredge scallops in flour mixture. Dip scallops in egg white, and dredge in flour mixture again.

Coat a large nonstick skillet with cooking spray; add 2 teaspoons margarine. Place over medium-high heat until margarine melts. Add half of scallops; cook 6 to 8 minutes or until scallops are lightly browned, turning to brown all sides. Remove scallops from skillet; set aside, and keep warm. Repeat procedure with remaining 2 teaspoons margarine and scallops. Wipe drippings from skillet with a paper towel.

Add wine and remaining 3 ingredients to skillet; cook 3 minutes or until mixture reduces to ¼ cup. Arrange scallops on a large serving platter; spoon sauce evenly over scallops. Yield: 6 servings.

PER SERVING: 185 CALORIES (14% FROM FAT)
FAT 2.8G (SATURATED FAT 0.3G)
PROTEIN 22.5G   CARBOHYDRATE 16.5G
CHOLESTEROL 37MG   SODIUM 285MG

GARLICKY BAKED SHRIMP

Vegetable cooking spray
1¼ pounds unpeeled medium-size fresh shrimp
½ cup fine, dry breadcrumbs
3 tablespoons finely chopped fresh parsley
1 teaspoon grated lemon rind
¼ teaspoon salt
3 cloves garlic, minced
2 tablespoons fresh lemon juice
1 tablespoon plus 1 teaspoon olive oil

Coat 4 individual gratin dishes with cooking spray. Peel and devein shrimp; divide shrimp evenly among dishes, and set aside.

Combine breadcrumbs, parsley, lemon rind, salt, and garlic in a bowl; stir in lemon juice and oil. Sprinkle breadcrumb mixture evenly over shrimp. Place dishes on a baking sheet. Bake at 400° for 13 minutes or until shrimp turn pink and breadcrumbs are lightly browned. Yield: 4 servings.

PER SERVING: 220 CALORIES (30% FROM FAT)
FAT 7.3G (SATURATED FAT 1.1G)
PROTEIN 24.7G   CARBOHYDRATE 12.5G
CHOLESTEROL 170MG   SODIUM 431MG

Fat Tip-Off

Good news for shrimp lovers! The American Heart Association says it's okay to eat shrimp. Although shrimp contain higher levels of cholesterol than some seafood, they are low in both total fat and saturated fat.

A 4-ounce serving of boiled or steamed shrimp contains only 1.2 grams of fat and 221 milligrams of cholesterol. (The AHA recommends limiting cholesterol to 300 milligrams a day.) So the next time you consider broiling a T-bone steak (at 24 grams of fat for 4 ounces), think shrimp instead.

Shrimp Monterey

SHRIMP MONTEREY

2¼ pounds unpeeled medium-size fresh
    shrimp
Vegetable cooking spray
1½ tablespoons chopped fresh cilantro
3 tablespoons all-purpose flour
1¼ cups skim milk, divided
1½ tablespoons reduced-calorie margarine
½ cup (2 ounces) shredded reduced-fat
    Monterey Jack cheese
1 jalapeño pepper, seeded and chopped
1 tablespoon grated Parmesan cheese
Fresh cilantro sprigs (optional)

Peel and devein shrimp; arrange shrimp in a steamer basket over boiling water. Cover and steam 3 minutes or until shrimp turn pink. Divide among 6 (1½-cup) baking dishes coated with cooking spray. Sprinkle with chopped cilantro; set aside.

Combine flour and ¼ cup milk in a small saucepan; stir until smooth. Add remaining 1 cup milk and margarine to flour mixture, stirring well. Cook over medium heat, stirring constantly, until mixture is thickened and bubbly. Remove from heat; add Monterey Jack cheese and jalapeño pepper, stirring until cheese melts.

Pour sauce evenly over shrimp; sprinkle evenly with Parmesan cheese. Broil 5½ inches from heat (with electric oven door partially opened) 3 to 5 minutes or until lightly browned. Garnish with fresh cilantro sprigs, if desired. Yield: 6 servings.

PER SERVING: 161 CALORIES (29% FROM FAT)
FAT 5.1G (SATURATED FAT 1.8G)
PROTEIN 22.1G   CARBOHYDRATE 5.1G
CHOLESTEROL 165MG   SODIUM 310MG

INDEX

METRIC EQUIVALENTS

Metric Equivalents for Different Types of Ingredients

A standard cup measure of a dry or solid ingredient will vary in weight depending on the type of ingredient. A standard cup of liquid is the same volume for any type of liquid. Use the following chart when converting standard cup measures to grams (weight) or milliliters (volume).

Standard Cup	Fine Powder (ex. flour)	Grain (ex. rice)	Granular (ex. sugar)	Liquid Solids (ex. butter)	Liquid (ex. milk)
1	140 g	150 g	190 g	200 g	240 ml
¾	105 g	113 g	143 g	150 g	180 ml
⅔	93 g	100 g	125 g	133 g	160 ml
½	70 g	75 g	95 g	100 g	120 ml
⅓	47 g	50 g	63 g	67 g	80 ml
¼	35 g	38 g	48 g	50 g	60 ml
⅛	18 g	19 g	24 g	25 g	30 ml

Useful Equivalents for Liquid Ingredients by Volume

¼ tsp					=	1 ml	
½ tsp					=	2 ml	
1 tsp					=	5 ml	
3 tsp	=	1 tbls		=	½ fl oz	=	15 ml
		2 tbls	=	⅛ cup	=	1 fl oz	=	30 ml
		4 tbls	=	¼ cup	=	2 fl oz	=	60 ml
		5⅓ tbls	=	⅓ cup	=	3 fl oz	=	80 ml
		8 tbls	=	½ cup	=	4 fl oz	=	120 ml
		10⅔ tbls	=	⅔ cup	=	5 fl oz	=	160 ml
		12 tbls	=	¾ cup	=	6 fl oz	=	180 ml
		16 tbls	=	1 cup	=	8 fl oz	=	240 ml
		1 pt	=	2 cups	=	16 fl oz	=	480 ml
		1 qt	=	4 cups	=	32 fl oz	=	960 ml
					33 fl oz	=	1000 ml = 1 l

Useful Equivalents for Dry Ingredients by Weight

(To convert ounces to grams, multiply the number of ounces by 30.)

1 oz	=	¹⁄₁₆ lb	=	30 g
4 oz	=	¼ lb	=	120 g
8 oz	=	½ lb	=	240 g
12 oz	=	¾ lb	=	360 g
16 oz	=	1 lb	=	480 g

Useful Equivalents for Cooking/Oven Temperatures

	Fahrenheit	Celcius	Gas Mark
Freeze Water	32° F	0° C	
Room Temperature	68° F	20° C	
Boil Water	212° F	100° C	
Bake	325° F	160° C	3
	350° F	180° C	4
	375° F	190° C	5
	400° F	200° C	6
	425° F	220° C	7
	450° F	230° C	8
Broil			Grill

Useful Equivalents for Length

(To convert inches to centimeters, multiply the number of inches by 2.5.)

1 in					=	2.5 cm	
6 in	=	½ ft			=	15 cm	
12 in	=	1 ft			=	30 cm	
36 in	=	3 ft	=	1 yd	=	90 cm	
40 in					=	100 cm	= 1 m